The New Guide to
Horse
Breeds

*The complete reference to horse and
pony breeds of the world*

J U D I T H
D R A P E R

Photography by
Kit Houghton

SMITHMARK

This edition published in 1997 by
Smithmark Publishers, a division of
U.S. Media Holdings, Inc.,
16 East 32nd Street,
New York, NY 10016

Smithmark Books are available for bulk purchase for sales
promotion and for premium use. For details write or call the
Manager of Special Sales, Smithmark Publishers,
16 East 32nd Street, New York, NY 10016; (212) 532-6600.

ISBN 0 7651 9524 0

Produced by Anness Publishing Limited
Hermes House
88-89 Blackfriars Road
London SE1 8HA

Previously published as part of a larger compendium,
The Book of Horses and Horse Care.

Publisher Joanna Lorenz
Senior editor Clare Nicholson
Project editor Marion Paull
Designer Michael Morey
Illustrator Rodney Paull

Printed in Singapore by Star Standard Industries Pte. Ltd.

1 3 5 7 9 10 8 6 4 2

❚ PAGE ONE: **Shagya Arab**
❚ PAGE TWO: **An Arab horse**
❚ PAGE FOUR: **Palomino**
❚ PAGE FIVE: **Vladimir Heavy Draught**
❚ PAGE SIX: **Horses at the Catherston Stud**

Contents

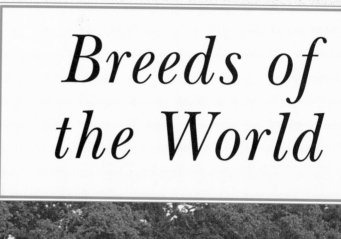

Breeds of
the World

Introduction

The lives of humans and horses have been bound together for many thousands of years. Appreciated first as just another source of food, the predecessors of the modern horse were hunted like any other wild animal. In time there came a steady process of domestication as nomadic peoples began to herd horses in the same way as they did goats and other animals. Ultimately, however, it was as a means of swift transport that the horse really came into his own. Men learnt to ride. Their whole lives were transformed. Horses became their chief means of transportation, remaining so until well into the twentieth century. Domestication, coupled with a gradual increase in human population, signalled the end of the truly wild horse. Today, even those horses which live in herds on the few remaining extensive areas of suitable grassland are not truly wild, for they are all "managed" by humans to one degree or another. Nevertheless horses retain much of the instinctive behaviour which enabled them to exist without man's intervention and it is necessary to understand what makes them "tick" if we are to enjoy our continuing association with them.

The History of the Horse

The modern horse, *Equus caballus*, belongs to the family *Equidae*, which also includes asses and zebras. *Equidae* are placed in the order Perissodactyla, to which tapirs and rhinoceroses belong and which descended from the Condylarthra, a group of primitive, long extinct mammals which were the ancestors of all hoofed mammals.

Fossil remains have made it possible to trace at least some aspects of the evolution of the modern horse over a period of some sixty million years, indicating how it gradually adapted to changes in its environment. The known history of the modern horse starts with Eohippus, also called the Dawn Horse, which is known to have lived in North America during the Eocene epoch (fifty-four to thirty-eight million years ago). An animal no larger than a small dog, Eohippus was designed for life as a forest browser moving around on soft soil. It had four toes on its forefeet, three on its back feet and pads similar to a dog's. Its small, low-crowned teeth were

■ PREVIOUS PAGE OPPOSITE
A Cleveland Bay.

■ PREVIOUS PAGE
A Furioso.

■ LEFT
The zebra is one of the small group of animals belonging to the family *Equidae*.

■ BELOW LEFT
The Highland Pony probably resembles Pony Type 2 of pre-domestication times.

■ BELOW RIGHT
The wiry Akhal-Teke is thought to approximate to Horse Type 3.

suited to eating leaves and other low, soft vegetation. It would probably have had a camouflage colouring to help it to escape predators. During the Oligocene epoch (thirty-seven to twenty-six million years

ago) first Mesohippus then Merychippus, showed distinct changes: the legs became longer, the back straighter (Eohippus had an arched back) and the whole animal larger. One toe disappeared on the forefoot, leaving three toes on both fore and hindfeet. The teeth also showed signs of change, the pre-molars becoming more like true molars.

In this slow process of evolution, the most significant change of all occurred during the Miocene epoch (twenty-five to seven million years ago) when forests gave

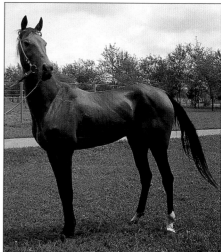

■ RIGHT
Horse Type 4 resembled this refined little Caspian
Pony. The Caspian was "re-discovered" in 1965.

■ RIGHT
Horse Type 4 resembled this refined little Caspian
Pony. The Caspian was "re-discovered" in 1965.

■ BELOW RIGHT
Pony Type 1 lived in north-west Europe and looked
like the present-day Exmoor Pony.

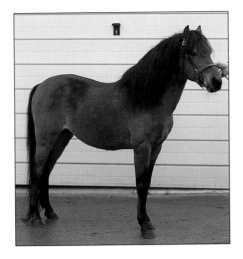

way to grassland and the horse's ancestors became plains dwellers. This significant change in environment called for teeth designed for grazing, as opposed to browsing, a longer neck to make grazing easier, longer legs to facilitate flight from predators and feet suitable for harder terrain. During this time the single toe, or hoof, began to evolve: the outer toes no longer touched the ground and the central toe became larger and stronger.

Then the history of the horse family becomes somewhat more complex, with various sub-families developing. Eventually, however, these became extinct and it was Pliohippus which provided the link in the chain from Eohippus to the modern Equus. Pliohippus evolved some ten to five million years ago and had long legs with a single hoof on each. Its direct successor, Equus, the genus of modern horse, finally emerged a million years ago.

During the Ice Ages of the Pleistocene epoch, Equus migrated via the land bridges which then existed to Europe, Asia and Africa. However, the disappearance of these land bridges (e.g. across what are now the Strait of Gibraltar and the Bering Strait) when the ice receded about 10,000 years ago meant that if an animal had become extinct in one continent, that

continent could not be repopulated – at least not without the help of man. This is exactly what happened in America: for some unexplained reason the horse disappeared. It was not seen again until European colonists reintroduced it thousands of years later.

All members of the modern *Equidae* family are swift runners with only one functional toe on each foot (the modern horse's ergot – the horny growth at the back of the fetlock – is believed to be the

vestiges of the pad of its ancestor, Eohippus). All live in herds and all have cheek teeth designed to grind plant-food.

Present-day horses and ponies are said to trace back to three distinct types, produced by variations in their natural environment. Northern Europe provided a slow-moving, heavy horse *(Equus silvaticus)* from which the world's heavy horse breeds are derived. Then there was the primitive Asiatic Wild Horse, survivors of which were found still living wild as late as 1881 (and called the Przewalski Horse); and finally the rather more refined Tarpan, from eastern Europe.

Later on, by the time that man began domesticating the horse, four sub-species had evolved: two pony types and two horse types. Pony Type 1 inhabited the north-west of Europe and resembled the modern Exmoor Pony. Pony Type 2, which was bigger and more heavily built, lived in northern Eurasia. The Highland Pony is probably the nearest modern-day equivalent. Horse Type 3 was a little bigger still, but much more lightweight in build and suited to hot climates. Its nearest equivalent is thought to be the Akhal-Teke. Horse Type 4, found in western Asia, was the smallest but the most refined and was the forerunner of the Caspian Pony.

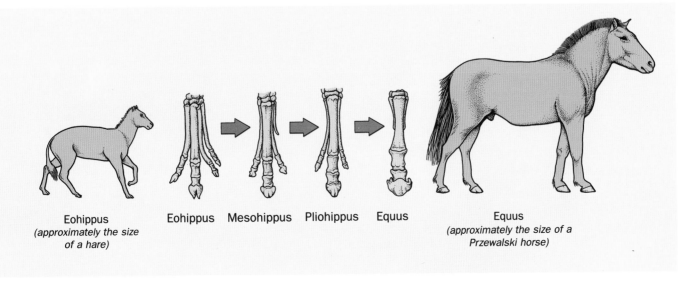

Eohippus
(approximately the size of a hare)

Eohippus   Mesohippus   Pliohippus   Equus

Equus
(approximately the size of a Przewalski horse)

Horses in the Wild

The horse is a herbivore, that is, an eater of plants. Like all herbivores horses are basically grass eaters. In the wild the horse is a nomadic grazer and spends up to twenty hours out of every twenty-four grazing. When food is plentiful a wild horse thrives and puts on weight; when it is scarce, and weather conditions harsh, he loses condition. Nature, as usual, has arranged for foals to be born in the spring when the weather is mild and the grass lush – thus ensuring that the mares have a plentiful supply of food, which in turn ensures ample milk for the foals. Mares come into season every twenty-one days during the spring and summer, until around September or October, and the gestation period is approximately eleven months.

Horses are by nature herd animals. In the wild they live in social groups within a larger group (the herd), each small group comprising a stallion, some mares, their foals and yearlings and perhaps one or two two-year-olds. Depending on the power of the stallion, the total size of the group is usually in the region of a dozen. Young, timid stallions and old ones who no longer have any mares often live in bachelor groups – horses do not like to be alone. Just as family life is important to them, so is friendship. Horses indulge in mutual grooming with their teeth, they play together and relax and doze together. A stallion will groom a favourite mare even when she is not in season (grooming is also used to stimulate a mare sexually) and will play with the foals – though eventually he will drive out the more mature colts who must then either join a bachelor group or begin to collect their own band of mares.

Horses communicate with each other by a number of means, both vocal and physical. Their "vocabulary" includes neighing, nickering, squealing and, more rarely, roaring. A loud neigh enables a horse to make contact with another from whom it has been separated; a quieter, lower nicker may be used by a stallion to a mare, a mare to her foal or between friends as a greeting; squeals are signs of excitement and are used when horses are in close contact, particularly sexual contact; horses may emit loud roars and

■ LEFT
This Dartmoor Pony is typical of a number of breeds which, although they have been domesticated for a very long time, have retained the ability to thrive in semi-wild conditions.

▌ LEFT
Horses are constantly on the alert. These semi-feral Camargue mares are aware of everything going on around them.

screams during a fight that has serious intentions, as opposed to the sort of play-fighting indulged in by young colts, and a mare may well scream her disapproval at a stallion who pesters her when she is not ready to be mated.

Body posture is another means of communication. A relaxed horse looks relaxed: a hind foot resting, head lowered, eyes partly closed, lower lip drooping. An excited stallion prances around, head tucked in, tail raised, his whole outline saying "look at me". A startled horse looks tense and alert, signs which indicate to its companions that there is cause for alarm.

Smell is also important to horses. Mares and foals recognize each other by smell. When meeting, horses will put their noses close together, often blowing down their nostrils, before deciding whether or not to be friends. Smell also plays a part in sexual communication – a stallion smells the vulva and urine of an in-season mare and can tell the difference between the dung of another stallion and that of a mare (he will urinate over a mare's dung but add his own dung to that left by a stallion).

A horse's ears, too, being tremendously mobile, say a good deal about what he is thinking – where his attention is focused, what mood he is in. Drooping ears indicate that the horse is in a dozy state, alert ones that something has caught his attention; ears that are turned back may show that the horse's attention is focused behind him or they may indicate submission or fear; ears laid flat denote anger or fear.

Having eyes set on the sides of his head, the horse can see almost all round him, the only blind spots being immediately behind and a little way in front of his head – he can keep an approaching object in focus merely by turning his head slightly. The horse's sense of touch is enhanced by the whiskers on his muzzle which enable him to judge how far an object is from the end of his nose and may also be useful for assessing texture, for example when he is grazing.

The horse's long legs enable him to travel at speed, essential for an animal whose natural form of defence is to run away. Since he is not equipped to fight predators such as wolves, lions and snakes, his chief means of survival is flight. This helps to explain why domesticated horses often prefer to shelter from bad weather by standing by a hedge or wall rather than making use of a specially provided man-made building: horses feel safer in the open air where they can easily gallop off if anything frightens them.

▌ LEFT
All horses and ponies are by nature herd animals, living in small social groups comprising a stallion, his mares and various offspring.

▌ RIGHT
Nature has equipped the Shetland Pony to withstand harsh winter weather. The thick coat ensures that the pony stays warm and the skin never gets wet.

Conformation

Conformation, or the horse's overall make and shape, varies a good deal from breed to breed. What constitutes "ideal" conformation varies according to the work which the horse is required to perform. In spite of these necessary variations, however, certain guidelines can be followed when looking for desirable conformation. They relate to proportion: if a horse is correctly proportioned he will be better balanced, less prone to unsoundness and more able to perform his allotted tasks than a horse with less harmonious proportions. Indeed, many a horse with conformational defects has been condemned as "difficult" when it is simply his shape which prevents him from carrying out what his master requires.

A horse is deemed to have "correct" proportions when certain measurements are equal. For example: the length of the head, the depth of the body at the girth,

the distance from the point of the hock to the ground, the distance from the chestnut on the foreleg to the ground, the distance from the croup to the fold of the stifle and from the fold of the stifle to the point of the hock should all be the same.

The domesticated horse is required to work, which means that certain features of his conformation are of particular importance. If a horse is deep through the girth, that is from the top of the wither to below the elbow, then his lungs will have plenty of room to expand – essential for any working horse. The length of his back is also important, particularly for the ridden horse. Too long, and it will be inclined to weakness; too short, and it may restrict the action.

Starting at the front, it is important that the horse's head is in proportion to his overall size. An over-large, heavy head will upset the overall balance, putting

extra weight on the forehand, which already carries 60 per cent of the horse's total weight. Too small a head will also affect the balance. The upper and lower jaws should meet evenly at the front – if they do not this will inhibit the horse's ability to bite food such as grass. The nostrils should be large and wide, and large eyes are preferable to small ones, which experience has shown often denote a less than generous temperament. The set of the head is also important. If there is not sufficient clearance between the mandible (the lower jaw) and the atlas (the top bone in the neck), the horse will have difficulty in flexing at the poll, a requirement in the more collected gaits. There should be room for two fingers' width when the horse's head is raised.

In the riding horse the neck should be fairly long and curved. There should be no tendency to fleshiness around the

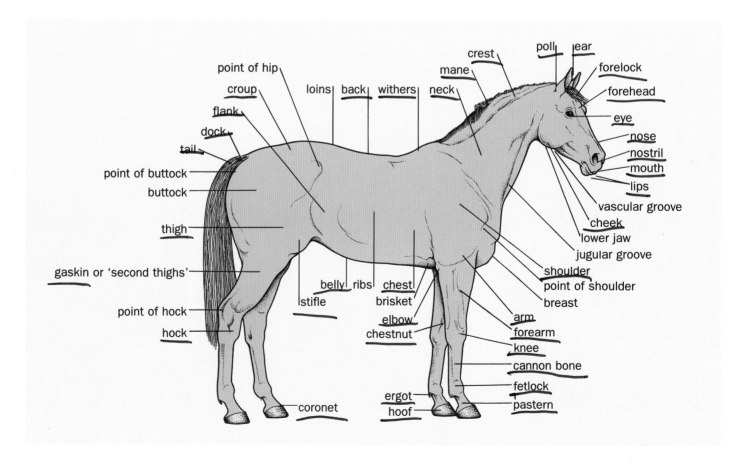

rounded and look like a matching pair. "Boxy" upright feet are prone to jarring. Large, flat feet may be more prone to bruising of the sole and to corns. The hindfeet, which bear less of the horse's overall weight when he is stationary, should be more oval in shape than the forefeet. Viewed from the side the slope of both fore and hindfeet should be a continuation of the slope of the pastern. The feet should point directly forwards.

throat, which again would restrict the flexion of the head. This is particularly important in the riding horse. A long neck is associated with speed, a shorter one with strength. Hence the heavy draught breeds lack the length of neck seen, for instance, in the Thoroughbred. The shoulder should be well sloped (the angle of the scapula gives the slope). Such conformation enables the horse to take longer strides than a straight shoulder, which results in short, restricted action. A straight shoulder may produce jarring, which can be detrimental to the forelimb. Horses with straight shoulders tend to give an uncomfortable ride, too. The shoulder should be muscular but not "loaded", i.e. too heavy. The withers should be of a good height and well defined. If they are too high, it may be difficult to fit a saddle. If they are poorly defined, it may be difficult to keep a saddle in place. With the draught horse, which must wear a collar and for whom pulling power is more important than extended paces, a slightly straighter shoulder is acceptable.

The chest and body should be reasonably broad, but not excessively so, otherwise the horse's movement will be affected. Narrowness in the chest, giving the forelegs the appearance of "coming out of one hole" is a serious fault, causing the foreleg joints to brush against each other. The back should rise slightly to the croup, and be well muscled. Short, well-muscled loins are essential: the lumbar

vertebrae have no support from the ribs, yet it is the loins which transfer the thrust from the engine (the hindquarters) to the body. The croup of the fully grown horse should be the same height as the withers and should not be too sloping, a feature which, combined with a low-set tail, is usually a sign of weakness. Croup-high horses throw extra weight on to the forehand, thus putting more strain on the forelimbs.

The horse's engine is in the back, that is in the hindquarters. They should therefore be strong and muscular. When standing still the hindlegs should not be stretched out behind him or tucked under him – a line dropped vertically from the point of the buttock to the ground should touch the hock and run down the rear of the cannon bone.

The forelegs should be straight and strong, with long, muscular forearms and large, flat knees. Short cannons indicate strength and there should be a good measurement of bone (the measurement being taken around the cannon below the knee). The amount of bone determines the weight-carrying ability of the horse. The amount of bone varies with the type of horse but as a rough guide a lightweight riding horse standing 16.2hh should have a minimum of 8 inches (20cm) of bone, a heavyweight horse of the same height at least 9 inches (23cm).

The pasterns should be of medium length and slope. The forefeet should be

COMMON CONFORMATIONAL DEFECTS

Back at the knee – where the knees, when viewed from the side, tend to extend backwards.

Calf knees – knees which are shallow from front to back.

Cow hocks – hocks which, when viewed from behind, turn inwards, as in a cow.

Ewe neck – where the top line of the neck is concave and the lower line convex.

Herring-gutted – where the horse has an upward slope from front to back on the underside of the belly.

Over at the knee – where the knees protrude forwards.

Pigeon toes – toes which turn inwards.

Roach back – where the spine has an exaggerated upward curve.

Sickle hocks – hocks which when viewed from the side have a concave line in front of the hocks and a slanting cannon bone.

Slab-sided – where the ribs are flat as opposed to "well-sprung".

Splay-footed – where the toes turn outwards.

Sway back – where the back has an exaggerated hollow.

Tied in below the knee – where the measurement of bone just below the knee is less than that farther down the cannon bone.

Colours and Markings

Equine coat colouring is controlled by numerous genes acting in combination to produce a multitude of variations in pigmentation. These genes, which are inherited, are located on paired structures known as chromosomes: the modern horse has 64 chromosomes, half of which are inherited from the sire and the other half from the dam. Some genes are dominant, others are recessive. For example, in horses chestnut is recessive to all other colours, bay is dominant to black, and grey is dominant to bay and black. The dominant greying gene can result in horses which are born with a dark coat turning progressively more grey as they

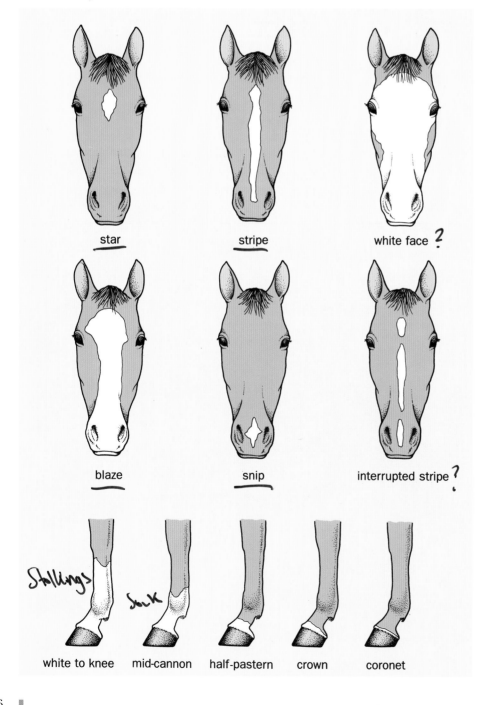

star

stripe

white face ?

blaze

snip

interrupted stripe ?

Stockings

sock

white to knee   mid-cannon   half-pastern   crown   coronet

FACIAL MARKINGS

These include: Star, stripe and interrupted stripe, snip, blaze, white face, white muzzle

LEG MARKINGS

For registration purposes leg markings are described in detail, using points of the anatomy: e.g. white to fetlock, white to knee, white to hock, etc.

Two less specific terms are also in popular use: sock (white colouring from the coronet up to the knee), stocking (white colouring from the coronet up to and over the knee or hock).

HOOF COLOURS

The horn of the hoofs can vary from blue or black to white and may be marked with dark stripes.

grow older. This is especially noticeable in the Lipizzaner, whose foals are born dark and, with rare exceptions, turn grey as they mature. Albinos occur where there is a congenital deficiency of colouring pigment. The hair is white, the skin pink and eyes often blue.

A horse is always described by its coat colouring, followed by other distinguishing features, where applicable, such as white markings and the colour of the mane and tail.

Some horses have more than one clearly defined coat colour. Broken or part-coloured horses such as piebalds and skewbalds (known as Pintos or Paint Horses in America) have irregular patches of two different colours while Spotted Horses show a variety of spotted markings. Black legs go with bay body colouring.

Horses' eyes are normally dark, although blue eyes also occur.

EQUINE COLOURS

Grey A mixture of black and white hairs throughout. The coat varies from light to iron (very dark). The skin is black.

Fleabitten Grey Grey coat flecked with brown specks.

Dappled Grey Light grey base coat with dark grey rings.

Bay Reddish coat with black mane, tail and "points" (i.e. limbs). The coat colour may vary from red to brown or yellowish.

Black All black except for occasional white marks on the legs and/or head.

Chestnut Varies from a pale golden colour to a rich, red gold. The mane and tail may be lighter or darker than the coat colour.

Liver Chestnut The darkest of the chestnut shades.

Sorrel A light-red chestnut.

Brown A mixture of black and brown hairs, with black limbs, mane and tail. A very dark brown horse may appear almost black.

Roan A body colour with white hairs interspersed, which lightens the overall effect.

Strawberry Roan Chestnut body colour with white hair giving a pinkish-red tinge.

Blue Roan Black or brown body colour with white hair giving a blue tinge.

Dun Light sandy-coloured coat with black mane and tail, often accompanied by a dark, dorsal eel-stripe extending from the line of the neck to the tail, and sometimes by "zebra markings" (stripes) on the withers and legs – the vestiges of a primitive form of camouflage. Dun can vary from yellow to "mouse", depending on the diffusion of pigment. The skin is black.

Palomino Gold coat with white mane and tail.

Spotted Small, more or less circular patches of hair of a different colour from the main body colour and distributed over various areas of the body.

Piebald Large, irregular patches of black and white.

Skewbald Large, irregular patches of white and any other colour except black.

Cream Cream-coloured coat with unpigmented skin (also known as cremello).

White Markings White markings on the face and legs and, occasionally, on the body, are a valuable means of distinguishing one horse from another and are therefore noted in detail on veterinary certificates and registration papers.

Brindle Brown or grey streaked or patched with a darker colour.

 OPPOSITE
ABOVE
The predominant coat colour of the Lipizzaner is grey, but foals are born dark and it takes several years for the coat to change to the typical "white" colouring associated with the breed.

RIGHT
Spotted coat patterns have existed – and often been highly prized – throughout man's long relationship with the horse. Spotted horses are particularly associated with the Nez Percé Indians of North America.

Horses

There are more than 150 different breeds and types of horses in the world. The development of each of them has been influenced by man. Domestication resulted in selective breeding and, in many instances, more nutritious feeding, both of which led to an increase in the size or the quality (or both) of the horse. However, the biggest influencing factor was the work which humans required their particular horses to perform. Those who needed to move heavy loads bred for strength, while others in need of fast transportation bred for speed. The terms coldblood and warmblood (which have nothing to do with temperature) are used to describe horses. Coldblood refers to the heavy draught breeds which are believed to be descended from the prehistoric horse of northern Europe. Warmblood refers to the lighter, riding type of horse. Nowadays the term "warmblood" is used in connection with the horses being bred for competition riding. The breeds in this book are organized by continent, then subdivided into countries within each continent.

"Wild" Horses

PRZEWALSKI HORSE

The horse no longer exists as a truly wild animal, although the Asiatic Wild Horse, believed to be one of the precursors of the domesticated horse, can still be seen in zoos in various parts of the world. The Asiatic Wild Horse *(Equus przewalskii przewalskii Poliakoff)* was "discovered" – or rather a small herd was – as recently as 1881 in the Tachin Schara Nuru Mountains on the edge of the Gobi desert by the Russian explorer Colonel N.M. Przewalski. Before that it was believed to have been extinct, over-hunted for its meat by Mongolian tribesmen. The Przewalski Horse, as it is widely known, differs genetically from the domesticated

horse, having 66 chromosomes instead of 64. In appearance it has several "primitive" features: a large head, with the eyes set high up rather than to the side of the head as in the case of the modern horse;

long ears; thick neck; heavy body with a dark dorsal strip and zebra markings on the legs. The Przewalski stands about 12–13hh and is always yellowish dun with a light-coloured nose and dark mane and

■ ABOVE
These Kaimanawa horses live in feral herds in New Zealand's North Island. Like the Brumbies of Australia they are unpopular with stockmen because they compete for food with domestic animals

■ PREVIOUS PAGE OPPOSITE

A Mustang.

■ PREVIOUS PAGE
A Trakehner.

■ LEFT
The Asiatic Wild Horse or Przewalski Horse is the only surviving race of the species from which domestic horses are descended. Its chromosome count differs from that of the domesticated horse.

tail. The mane, which grows upright, is shed each spring and there is no forelock. Intractable by nature – it cannot be trained for riding – the Przewalski can survive on a minimum of food and endure extremes of heat and cold.

TARPAN

Eastern Europe and European Russia were the home of the Tarpan, another horse widely believed to have been an ancestor of the modern horse. It survived in the wild until the nineteenth century. One authority claims that the last true Tarpan in captivity died in 1919, in which case the Tarpan which exists today, running semi-wild in reserves in Poland, must be a "reconstruction", almost certainly bred from the Konik, which it strongly resembled. Experiments with crossing Przewalski stallions and Konik mares have also produced an animal which looks very like the original Tarpan. The Tarpan was (and is) more lightly built than the Przewalski, standing about 13hh and with

a brown or mouse dun coat, dark mane and tail and, frequently, primitive dorsal stripe and zebra markings.

BRUMBY

Australia's "wild" horse, the Brumby, is not a true wild horse, equine animals having been unknown in Australasia until the

arrival of European settlers a few hundred years ago (the assumption being that because there were no land bridges linking the Americas with Australia, Eohippus and its descendants had no means of migrating there). The Brumbies which live in feral herds in the Northern Territory and, to a lesser extent, in central Australia, are descended from settlers' horses who wandered off into the bush, producing offspring that grew up under wild conditions. When rounded up and broken in some Brumbies have, over the years, been useful to man but today they are generally regarded as a pest and are culled because they compete for food with domestic animals.

See also Camargue, Mustang, Sorraia.

▌ **ABOVE LEFT**
The primitive looking Konik pony is found in Poland and is a descendant of the Tarpan. Crossed with Przewalski stallions, Konik mares produce Tarpan "look-alikes".

▌ **LEFT**
The Sorraia pony, which can be found living in semi-feral conditions in Portugal, is believed to be of ancient origin.

Arabian

The oldest and purest of all horse breeds, the Arab is considered by many people to be the most beautiful equine animal in the world. With its refined head and dished profile, expressive eyes, high spirits and unique, floating action, it is undoubtedly one of the most exquisite of creatures. Although it has certainly been bred with great care for many centuries, its exact origins are unclear. Depictions of horses in ancient art suggest that horses of Arab type lived in the Arabian peninsula as long ago as 2,000 – 3,000BC. Like the desert tribes with whom they have lived for so long, Arab horses became superbly well adapted to life in a harsh environment, having extreme powers of endurance, tremendous soundness and the ability to thrive on the most meagre of rations.

More than any other horse, it is the Arab which has influenced the development of equine

BREED DESCRIPTION

Height 14.2 – 15hh.

Colour Predominantly chestnut, grey, bay and black.

Conformation Small head with broad forehead, fine muzzle, concave profile, wide nostrils and small ears; deep, clearly defined jowl with the throat set into it in a distinctly arched curve; graceful, curving neck; long, sloping shoulders with well-defined withers; deep, roomy body with broad, deep chest and short, level back; high-set tail; hard, clean limbs with well-defined tendons and dense, fine bone; hard, well-shaped feet; fine, silky mane and tail.

INTERESTING FACTS

The unique outline of the Arab is determined by the formation of its skeleton, which differs from other equine breeds in several respects. The Arab has 17 ribs (other horses have 18); five lumbar vertebrae (other horses have six), and 16 tail vertebrae (other horses have 18).

▌ TOP
Large eyes and nostrils are typical of the Arab. The short, refined head, with its dished profile, is one of the breed's most distinctive features.

▌ LEFT
The Arab's comparatively small size belies its weight-carrying ability. Standing no more than 15hh it will nevertheless carry a fully grown man with ease.

breeds throughout the world. This Arabian influence was initiated in the seventh and early eighth centuries AD when the followers of Islam spread across North Africa and into Spain. The horses they took with them were greatly superior to the native stock of other lands and so began a process of upgrading, through the introduction of Arab blood, that was to go on for many centuries and, indeed, still goes on today.

Pure-bred Arabian horses are now bred throughout the world. As well as appearing in the show ring, they are particularly suited to the sport of endurance riding. In recent times, too, there has been a resurgence of interest in Arab racing.

▌ ABOVE LEFT
The Arab horse often appears to float over the ground. This remarkable action, coupled with a gentle temperament, makes it a popular riding horse throughout the world.

▌ ABOVE RIGHT
The breed's legendary stamina makes it the perfect choice for endurance riding which at the top level involves covering a distance of 100 miles (161km) in a day.

▌ LEFT
With its elegance, spirit and exceptional looks, it is easy to see why the Arab is often considered to be the world's most beautiful horse.

Barb

The Barb comes from Morocco, Algeria and Tunisia – the coastal regions of these North African countries were formerly known as the Barbary Coast, "Barbary" meaning foreign or, more specifically, non-Christian lands. Opinions differ as to the Barb's origins, lack of documentary evidence making it impossible to do more than hazard an educated guess. According to one school of thought, the Barb may trace back to an isolated group of wild horses which survived the Ice Age. If that were true, it would make the Barb an even older breed than the Arab. Another theory links the Barb to the Akhal-Teke, the horse of the Turkmens.

Although it is unlikely that the breed's true origins will ever be revealed, what is certain is that the Barb has had more influence on the development of equine breeds throughout the world than any other horse except the Arab. As with the Arab, it was the spread of Islam which led to the forerunners of today's Barbs reaching Europe from the early eighth century onwards (the first Muslim army, seven thousand strong, landed in Spain in the spring of 711). Once established on the Iberian peninsula the Barb horse played a major role in the development of the Andalusian, which subsequently became one of the major influences in horse breeding all over the world. Among the many historical references to

BREED DESCRIPTION

Height Around 14.2 – 15.2hh.

Colour Predominantly grey, bay, brown and black.

Conformation Narrow head with convex profile; arched neck; flat shoulders with well-defined withers; short, strong body; sloping hindquarters with fairly low-set tail; rather slender, but strong, limbs; narrow, but hard, feet.

■ BELOW
The Barb lacks the refinement and elegance of the Arab but is equally tough and enduring.

"Barbary" horses perhaps the most famous is Roan Barbary, belonging to the English king, Richard II (1367–1400). During the sixteenth century Henry VIII imported a number of Barbary horses into England and a century later the Barb played an important part in the evolution of the Thoroughbred. Elsewhere the influence of the Barb is still evident in the Argentinian Criollo and the American Mustang.

Despite its importance as a progenitor of other breeds, the Barb has achieved less widespread renown than the Arab, no doubt because it lacks the Arab's unique visual appeal, being much less refined and generally less impressive in appearance. Nevertheless it has the same boundless stamina and endurance, the same ability to thrive on meagre rations, the same sure-footedness – and an impressive turn of speed over short distances.

Dressed in ceremonial attire, Barb horses and their
Moroçcan riders are a colourful sight at a modern
"Fantasia".

INTERESTING FACTS

The most well-known Barb horses of modern
times were those ridden by the Spahis, men
of the Algerian and Tunisian cavalry
regiments in the French army. The Spahis
originally came from Turkey but were
incorporated into their army by the French
when the latter occupied Algiers and Tunis.
Barb horses still feature in the exciting
present-day North African festivals recalling
these countries' military pasts.

■ BELOW
In the dramatic rifle-firing charge seen at North
African festivals, Barb horses demonstrate their
impressive speed over a short distance.

Andalusian

As its name suggests, the Andalusian comes from the sun-baked region of southern Spain which is close to North Africa. While it is without doubt an ancient breed, its origins are uncertain. Whatever native horses existed in Spain when the Muslim invaders arrived in 711 – they may well have resembled the primitive Sorraian Pony still found today in Portugal – must surely have been crossed subsequently with

the invaders' Barb horses, which were imported in such great numbers.

After the last Muslim state, Granada, had fallen to the Christians in 1492, Spain began to assume a new importance in the western world and so, too, did her horses. Taken to the Americas by the sixteenth-century

Conquistadores, Spanish horses provided the foundation stock for the majority of new breeds developed by the settlers. In Europe, meanwhile, the Spanish horse became the preferred mount of monarchs and of the great riding masters, including the Englishman, William Cavendish, Duke of Newcastle, who in the seventeenth century wrote that: "If well chosen it is the noblest horse in the world; the most beautiful that can be. He is of great spirit and of great courage and docile; has the proudest walk, the proudest trot...the loftiest gallop and is the lovingest and gentlest horse and fittest of all for a king in Day of Triumph." The Lipizzaner is a direct descendant of the Andalusian, while other famous European breeds influenced by Spanish blood include the Frederiksborg, the Friesian (which in turn

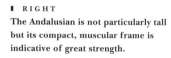

█ RIGHT
The Andalusian is not particularly tall but its compact, muscular frame is indicative of great strength.

BREED DESCRIPTION

Height 15 – 15.2hh.

Colour Predominantly grey (including "mulberry" – a dappled, purplish grey) and bay.

Conformation Handsome head with broad forehead and large, kind eyes; fairly long, thick but elegant neck; long, well-sloped shoulders with well-defined withers; short, strong body with broad chest and well-sprung ribs; very broad, strong, rounded hindquarters with rather low-set tail; medium length limbs, clean cut and elegant but strong; long and very luxuriant mane and tail.

horses aren't ment to be on the breed (handwritten note)

LEFT
On point duty in
present-day Barcelona.
Thanks to its excellent
temperament and
willing nature, the
Andalusian is an ideal
all-purpose riding
horse.

BELOW
Grey is one of the predominant Andalusian colours,
along with bay. Spotted strains were once popular
and were responsible for the founding of the
Appaloosa breed in America.

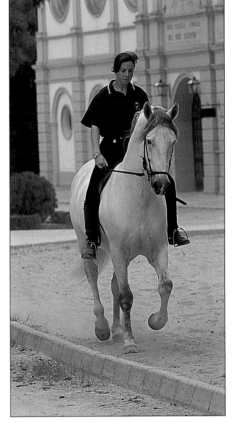

INTERESTING FACTS

The Andalusian horse's survival down the
centuries, which included some pretty
turbulent times, was aided by the monastic
orders, particularly the Carthusians, who
became especially skilful at horse breeding. In
times of danger, horses were moved from the
great studs to remote monasteries for safe
keeping. The Carthusians were instrumental in
maintaining purity of line and produced
animals of consistently high quality.

influenced the Oldenburg), the Holstein
and the Connemara.

The Andalusian is one of the most
elegant of horses. Possessing tremendous
presence, lofty paces, agility and a gentle,
willing nature, it makes an excellent
all-round riding horse and is particularly
well suited to the movements of the
haute école (high school). It can also be
seen to great effect taking part in the
colourful annual *ferias*, or fairs, of its
native Andalusia.

RIGHT
The breed's proud
bearing and lofty
action lend themselves
perfectly to the
movements of the
haute école, or high
school.

Thoroughbred

The life of man has been inextricably interwoven with that of the horse for more than 4,000 years but in all that time no achievement has excelled the "invention" of the Thoroughbred. Quite apart from being the world's supreme racehorse, the Thoroughbred has played a vital part in the upgrading of numerous old horse and pony breeds and in establishing as many new ones.

Henry VIII set the process in motion during the sixteenth century when he

founded the famous Royal Paddocks at Hampton Court. His daughter, Elizabeth I, founded another stud at Tutbury, in Staffordshire. Both monarchs imported horses from Spain and Italy to cross with native stock. Under subsequent monarchs – James I, Charles I and Charles II – horse breeding and racing gained impetus. By the beginning of the seventeenth century regular race meetings were being staged at Newmarket, Chester, Doncaster and Lincoln. Many noblemen took up the

▌ **ABOVE RIGHT**
The head of the Thoroughbred is typically refined, with large eyes and nostrils. The dished profile so characteristic of its Arabian forebears is not found in the Thoroughbred.

▌ **RIGHT**
With its well-sloped shoulders, powerful hindquarters and long limbs, the Thoroughbred is the ultimate "racing machine". The deep girth ensures plenty of room for the heart and lungs.

Stop slaughter
Stop racing
Stop!

■ RIGHT
The bigger, slower developing stamp of Thoroughbred often makes a first-rate steeplechaser. Chasing calls for courage, stamina and speed, qualities for which the Thoroughbred is renowned.

Stop! forever

■ BELOW RIGHT
Thanks to carefully kept records (in the *General Stud Book*) dating back some two centuries, it is possible to trace the pedigree of this foal to one of the breed's handful of foundation sires.

■ BOTTOM
Thoroughbreds hurdling at speed at Cheltenham, spiritual home of the sport of jump racing. The Thoroughbred's athletic prowess makes it equally suitable for sports such as hunting and three-day eventing.

breeding of horses for racing, sending agents overseas to seek out good stallions. Records of the time repeatedly refer to Barb, Barbary, Arabian, Hobby and Galloway horses (the Irish Hobby and Scottish Galloway were famous "running"' horses of the day) – and it is on this blood that the modern Thoroughbred was founded.

The exact breeding of the Thoroughbred's forebears will never be known since horses often changed names when they changed hands and the terms "Arabian", "Barb" and "Turk", were frequently used inaccurately. However, what is certain is that during the last quarter of the seventeenth century and the first quarter of the eighteenth, Englishmen or their agents bought a number of eastern stallions, crossed them with English mares of mixed pedigree and started a dynasty of great racehorses. The most famous of these stallions were the Byerley Turk, the Darley Arabian and the Godolphin Arabian, who are recognized as the founding fathers of the Thoroughbred. In 1791 *An Introduction to a General Stud Book* appeared and following the publication of several more preliminary editions, there came, in 1808, Volume I of the *General Stud Book*. A horse is classed as Thoroughbred if both its parents are entered in the *General Stud Book* (or in the equivalent official Thoroughbred stud books in other countries).

The Thoroughbred is a handsome horse, alert, spirited and full of presence. It has an easy, ground-covering stride at the gallop and possesses boundless courage and immense stamina, qualities which stand it in good stead on the racecourse, in the hunting field and in three-day eventing.

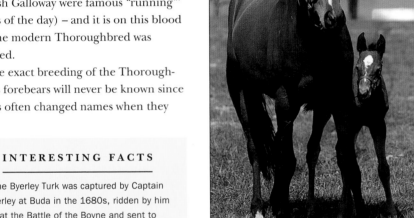

INTERESTING FACTS

The Byerley Turk was captured by Captain Byerley at Buda in the 1680s, ridden by him at the Battle of the Boyne and sent to England to stand at stud. His great-grandson Tartar sired Herod, one of the most important sires in Thoroughbred history. The Darley Arabian, foaled in 1700, was acquired by Thomas Darley and sent to England from the Syrian port of Aleppo. He was responsible for founding the Eclipse line – Eclipse was one of the greatest racehorses of all time. The Godolphin Arabian was foaled in the Yemen in 1724, exported to Tunis via Syria and later given by the Bey of Tunis to the King of France, who subsequently sold him to Edward Coke, from Derbyshire. He was eventually acquired by Lord Godolphin and was responsible for founding the Matchem line. The Herod, Eclipse and Matchem lines, plus the Highflyer (Highflyer was a son of Herod) are the four principal tail-male lines of the modern Thoroughbred.

Stop!

Anglo-Arab

A more substantial horse than the pure-bred Arab, the Anglo-Arab is produced by mixing Arab and Thoroughbred blood. The Anglo-Arab can result from a first cross between a Thoroughbred stallion and an Arab mare or vice versa. It can also be produced by breeding Thoroughbred to Anglo-Arab or Arab to Anglo-Arab, or Anglo-Arab to Anglo-Arab. As a result of these different permutations, the amount of Arab blood varies a good deal. So, too, does the size and appearance of the horse. The biggest horses are often produced by using an Arab stallion on a Thoroughbred mare and the best examples of the Anglo-Arab will inherit the endurance and stamina of the Arab and the speed and scope of the Thoroughbred, but not the latter's rather high-strung temperament.

France has been a notable producer of Anglo-Arabs since the first half of the nineteenth century. The French Anglo-Arab traces back to two eastern stallions, Massoud (an Arab) and Aslam (which is said to be of Turkish origin). They were imported from Syria and crossed with three imported English Thoroughbred

BREED DESCRIPTION

Height Around 15.3 – 16.3hh.

Colour Usually chestnut, bay or brown.

Conformation Variable, but the best specimens tend towards good Thoroughbred conformation: intelligent head with straight profile, expressive eyes and alert ears; long neck with more prominent withers than the Arab; sloping shoulders; short, strong body – rather more sturdy than the Thoroughbred – with deep chest; somewhat long hindquarters; good, sound limbs; strong, well-shaped feet.

▌ TOP LEFT
The head of the Anglo-Arab is closer in appearance to that of the Thoroughbred than the Arab. The Anglo lacks the dished profile of the pure-bred.

▌ LEFT
The overall conformation is noticeably more Thoroughbred than Arab, although many Anglo-Arabs are more sturdily built than the average Thoroughbred.

▌ LEFT
The crossing of Thoroughbred with Arab blood has produced some outstanding competition horses in the Olympic disciplines, including dressage.

mares, Daer, Comus Mare and Selim Mare. Their three daughters, Delphine, Clovis and Danaë became the foundation stock of France's first breed of sports horse. At one time the Anglo-Arab was much used in France by the military and as a general riding and competition horse. More recently it has been an influential factor in the development of the modern sports horse, the Selle Français.

▌ BELOW
In recent years French Anglo-Arabs such as this one have achieved great success in top-level three-day eventing, holding their own against the best of the Thoroughbreds and Warmbloods.

INTERESTING FACTS

Before the development of the Selle Français, the French Anglo-Arab was highly successful in the competitive disciplines, particularly show jumping. Many of the horses ridden by the dual Olympic champion Pierre Jonquères d'Oriola were Anglo-Arabs, the most famous being the little gelding Marquis III (a very successful Grand Prix and Nations' Cup horse) and Ali-Baba, on whom d'Oriola won his first Olympic title at Helsinki in 1952. More recently French Anglo-Arabs have been successful performers with the French three-day event team. They include Twist la Beige (winner of the European Championship in 1993) and Newport and Newlot (both European team silver medallists).

Noriker

Bred and developed over several thousand years in the mountain regions of Austria, the Noriker is an attractive looking light draught horse. Strong and hardy, this horse is noted particularly for its calm temperament, sound limbs and sure-footedness. These characteristics make it an ideal all-round work horse over difficult mountainous terrain.

As with most horses, despite its ancient origins there was no formal breeding programme until fairly recent times. The Prince-Archbishop of Salzburg is credited with forming a stud book some 400 years ago. It was then that standards were drawn up, for both mares and stallions, and stud farms established.

Because of its toughness and capacity for hard work the Noriker became popular throughout Europe. Different strains evolved, including the Bavarian, now known as the South German Coldblood and found in Upper and Lower Bavaria. Various colour lines, tracing back to Andalusian and Neapolitan horses, also had an influence on today's breed and were responsible for the dappled and brindle colourings.

BREED DESCRIPTION

Height Stallions 16 – 17hh.
Mares 15.3 – 17hh.

Colour Brown, chestnut, black, grey and brindle. White body markings are not acceptable. Too many or too large white markings on the head and limbs are not desirable.

Conformation Straight profile, wide nostrils, medium-sized eyes; medium-length neck with thick, curly mane; good sloping shoulders; broad, deep chest; medium-length, well-muscled back; long limbs with powerful forearms, large clean joints, well-muscled second thigh and good, sound feet.

INTERESTING FACTS

The breed takes its name from the ancient state of Noricum (during the Roman Empire Noricum was roughly approximate to present-day Austria). However, the Noriker can be traced back to pre-Roman times, when a heavy war horse was developed in Thessalonica. Horses of this type were taken to Noricum by the Romans. In due course they were crossed with other coldblooded horses of the region and became admirably adapted to the harsh conditions of their new environment.

▮ ABOVE
Most Norikers are brown but the breed embraces a wide range of coat colours, including this attractive dark chestnut with flaxen mane.

▮ LEFT
The Noriker's sturdy build and good limbs and feet make it an ideal work horse in mountainous regions. Like most mountain breeds, it is a good mover, with a particularly active trot.

Belgian Draught

One of the world's finest and historically most important heavy horses, the Belgian Draught is an ancient breed, closely connected to the Ardennais. The Flanders Horse, as the breed was known during the Middle Ages, had an influence on the development of several other renowned "heavies", including the Shire, the Suffolk Punch and particularly the Clydesdale. Nowadays the Belgian Draught is also known as the Brabant, after its main breeding area in central Belgium.

Despite widespread mechanization, this gentle giant of a horse, known for its kind nature and willingness to work, can still be found in modest numbers in many areas of Belgium and is also much appreciated in North America.

Over the years breeders have managed to maintain the excellence of these horses by a policy of strict selection and some inbreeding. The result is a handsome individual – its short neck, strong shoulders, short limbs, deep-girthed body and huge hindquarters, coupled with the most amenable of temperaments, make it the ideal draught horse for work on the land and there is no finer sight in the equestrian world than a team of these magnificent animals hitched to a smart brewers' dray.

▌ ABOVE
The Belgian Draught is an impressive horse, combining great strength with a gentle temperament and willingness to work. Despite its size, it is economical to keep.

BREED DESCRIPTION

Height 16.2 – 17hh.

Colour Predominantly red-roan with black points, chestnut and sorrel. Bay, dun and grey also occur.

Conformation Small, rather plain head but with intelligent expression; short, muscular neck; massive shoulders; short, deep, compact body; rounded, powerful hindquarters; short, strong limbs with plenty of feather and well-shaped, medium-sized feet.

INTERESTING FACTS

Towards the end of the last century there were three recognized types of Brabant horse, each based on a different bloodline. Those from the celebrated stallion Orange I, known as the Gros de la Dendre line, were mainly bay in colour. A stallion called Bayard founded the Gris du Hainaut line, with its greys, red-roans and sorrels. A third line, the Colosses de la Méhaigne, descended from the bay stallion Jean I. Today the descendants of these bloodlines all come under the general title of Belgian Draught or Brabant.

▌ ABOVE LEFT
The head is rather plain but the eyes have the kindly expression associated with so many of the heavy breeds.

▌ LEFT
Massive hindquarters are typical of the breed. These horses have docked tails.

Frederiksborg

The stud after which the Frederiksborg is named was founded by King Frederick II during the 1560s and was famous as a provider of quality horses to the courts of Europe. The stud's foundation stock came from Spain and was subsequently crossed with the Spanish horse's close relative, the Neapolitan. The horses thus produced were both elegant and spirited and well suited to the dual requirements of the day: as a mount for work in the manège and as a charger for the cavalry.

■ RIGHT
The Frederiksborg's somewhat plain head has a kind, intelligent look about it. Most examples of the breed, like this horse, are chestnut.

BREED DESCRIPTION

Height 15.3 – 16hh.

Colour Chestnut.

Conformation Intelligent, if somewhat plain, head; short, upright neck; strong but rather upright shoulders; strong back that tends to be long; high-set tail; good, strong feet.

The breed continued to develop through the introduction of eastern and British half-bred stallions and for several centuries the Frederiksborg was one of the most sought-after horses in Europe. Eventually, so numerous were the exports of the Frederiksborg from Denmark that stock became seriously depleted, with the result that during the first half of the nineteenth century the stud turned instead to Thoroughbred breeding. This venture was not a success and in 1871 the stud was dispersed. Fortunately, however, Frederiksborgs did not disappear altogether: private breeders went on producing them, mainly for use as light harness horses.

Frederiksborgs are still bred in Denmark, although recent demands for an outstanding sports horse have led to the development of a new horse, the Danish Warmblood, based mainly on Swedish, German and Polish stallions. Frederiksborg blood does occasionally appear in today's Danish Warmblood pedigrees, chiefly through the female line.

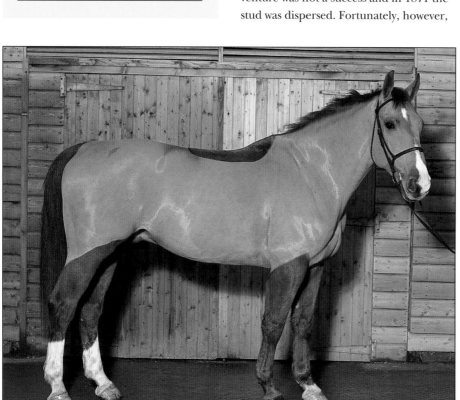

INTERESTING FACTS

The Frederiksborg played a significant part in the development of a much more well-known breed, the Lipizzaner, famous for its association with the Spanish Riding School in Vienna. The white stallion Pluto, from the Royal Danish Court Stud, was one of the six stallions on which the Lipizzaner breed is based. Pluto was foaled in 1765, the earliest of the six. More than two centuries later his descendants are still performing at the Spanish Riding School where they can be identified by the "Pluto" prefix to their names.

■ LEFT
The rather long back, short neck and upright shoulders are more typical of the light harness horse than the riding horse.

Jutland

Except for the feathering of its lower legs, Denmark's heavy horse bears an uncanny resemblance to the British breed, the Suffolk Punch. This resemblance is perhaps not so surprising, because the present-day Jutland was greatly influenced by the Suffolk blood introduced via the English stallion Oppenheim LXII, who stood at stud in Denmark during the 1860s.

The breed goes back much further than that, however. Heavy horses have been bred on the Jutland Peninsula for many centuries, certainly as far back as the twelfth century, when they were in great demand as war horses. Combining enormous strength with the most willing

BREED DESCRIPTION

Height 15 – 16hh.

Colour Predominantly dark chestnut with light mane and tail.

Conformation Heavy, rather plain head, but with kind expression; short, thick neck; strong, muscular shoulders; exceptionally deep body with broad chest; round, muscular hindquarters; short limbs with plenty of bone.

INTERESTING FACTS

The Jutland was an influential factor in the development of the Schleswig, a draught horse which takes its name from the northernmost region of Germany and which towards the end of the nineteenth century was in demand for pulling trams and buses. Infusions of Jutland blood from neighbouring Denmark were being used by German breeders well into this century. The Schleswig closely resembles the Jutland and the Suffolk, both in build and colour. However, the use of carefully selected Boulonnais and Breton stallions from France has led to the appearance of some greys and bays.

of natures, the Jutland horse made the ideal mount for the heavily armoured knights of the Middle Ages. Cleveland Bay and Yorkshire Coach Horse blood is said to have been used in the development of the Jutland, but it is unquestionably the Suffolk which has been the dominant factor, even to its chestnut colouring.

Mechanization has reduced the numbers of these attractive horses but some can still be seen, either at shows or pulling drays in the cities or, occasionally, working the land.

▌ ABOVE
In common with all heavy breeds, the handsome Jutland has been the victim of mechanization but a few are still working.

▌ LEFT
The Jutland is usually chestnut, a colour inherited through the Suffolk Punch element in its ancestry.

Danish Warmblood

The Danish Warmblood is one of a number of horses specifically developed for use in modern equestrian pursuits, particularly the competitive disciplines of dressage, show jumping and three-day eventing.

The Danes have a long tradition as horse breeders: their first organized studs date from the fourteenth century. However, the market for horses has changed enormously this century, and especially during the last few decades. In many countries the relentless march of mechanization has transformed the horse from an essential means of transport to a "leisure" animal. In the wake of this transformation the Danes found that their native breeds – the Frederiksborg and its cousin, the spotted Knabstrup (a popular circus horse) – were not going to measure up as competitive sports horses.

To remedy this deficiency, a breeding programme was set up in 1962 to produce a new type of Danish riding horse.

BREED DESCRIPTION

Height 15.3 – 16.3hh.

Colour All colours occur.

Conformation Quality head; long, well set-on neck; good shoulders with prominent withers; muscular back and loins; long croup; strong limbs with long forearms, well-defined joints and good bone.

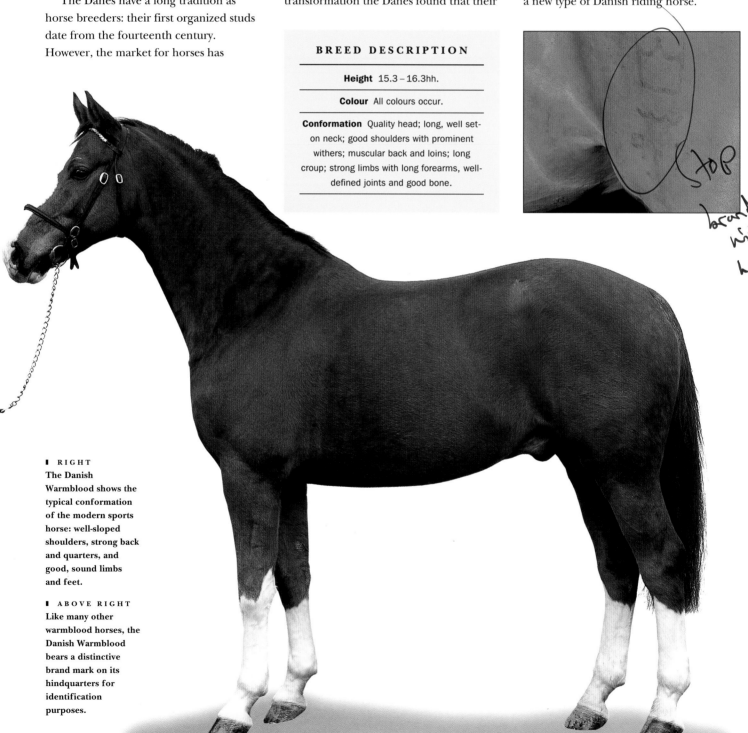

■ RIGHT
The Danish Warmblood shows the typical conformation of the modern sports horse: well-sloped shoulders, strong back and quarters, and good, sound limbs and feet.

■ ABOVE RIGHT
Like many other warmblood horses, the Danish Warmblood bears a distinctive brand mark on its hindquarters for identification purposes.

■ **ABOVE**
Warmblood horses
have been specifically
developed for use in
competitive sports
such as show jumping.

■ **ABOVE RIGHT**
A good deal of
German blood has
been used in the
development of the
Danish Warmblood.
This is reflected in its
quality head.

■ **RIGHT**
Perhaps the most
famous of all Danish
Warmbloods is the
dressage stallion
Matador, winner of the
silver medal at the
1990 World Equestrian
Games.

Carefully selected stallions, chiefly
Swedish, Trakehner, Hanoverian,
Holstein and Polish, were crossed with
the various local-bred mares to improve
the basic stamp of horse. Stringent
grading was introduced for both stallions
and mares to ensure that only the best
were granted entry to the stud books.
The breeding programme has been a
tremendous success. The resultant Danish
Warmblood is a handsome individual, well
proportioned and possessed of excellent
paces. It combines courage with a good
temperament and makes an outstanding
dressage horse.

Ariègeois

The Ariègeois, which lives in the Pyrenean mountains in the south-west of France, is a breed of great antiquity. It closely resembles the horses of southern Gaul described in Caesar's commentaries on

BREED DESCRIPTION

Height 13.1 – 14.3hh (the latter is rarely attained in its native habitat, although it may be on richer, lowland grazing).

Colour Solid black. Normally no white stockings or markings on the head, although the flank may be lightly flecked with white.

Conformation Light-boned, expressive head with flat forehead, straight profile, fairly short, hairy ears and bright, alert eyes with a gentle expression; fairly short, straight neck; rather straight shoulders; long but strong back and broad chest; round hindquarters with sloping croup; short, fairly slender limbs with a tendency to cow hocks; good, strong feet.

the Gallic Wars. Its home is the high valley of the Ariège river, from which it takes its name. Well adapted to the worst excesses of its mountain environment, it is impervious to cold and outstandingly sure-footed – ice-covered mountain trails hold no terrors for the little Ariègeois.

A versatile, hardy creature, the Ariègeois has for centuries been used as a packhorse, though it can just as easily function as a small riding horse or work the land on the steepest of hill farms, where modern machinery cannot venture.

INTERESTING FACTS

The coat of the Ariègeois acquires a distinctive reddish tinge in winter. It is fine in texture, unlike the mane and tail, which are harsh to the touch and extremely thick – nature's way of offering much-needed protection from the worst of the winter weather. The Ariègeois is less well suited to heat. In summer it will seek shelter from the sun during the hottest part of the day and come out to graze at night.

❙ TOP
Like all mountain breeds, the Ariègeois has very active paces. It has exceptionally strong hooves and is noted for its sure-footedness.

❙ LEFT
The Ariègeois has a fairly long, but nevertheless strong, back, a powerfully built neck and deep girth. The sloping croup and low-set tail are characteristic.

Norman Cob

The Norman Cob is a light draught horse, still in use on small farms in the La Manche region of Normandy. Normandy has long been famed for its horse breeding, notably at the historic studs of Le Pin (founded as a royal stud in the mid-seventeenth century) and Saint-Lô, where the ancestors of the modern Cob were bred.

Stocky and compact, like the English Cob after which it was named, the Norman Cob was developed as a distinct breed at the beginning of this century. It was at that time that the breeders of half-bred horses first began to distinguish between those animals suitable for use as riding horses, particularly for the army, and those of less quality and sturdier build, more suited to light draught work.

The Norman Cob, as the heavier type was subsequently named, became a popular workhorse, especially in the La Manche region – even the powerful Percheron failed to supplant it there.

Over the years there has been a tendency for the Norman Cob to become heavier, to cope with the work required of it, but although it is undoubtedly sturdy and muscular, it lacks the massive stature of the true heavy horse and has never lost the energetic action, particularly at trot, characteristic of the half-bred horse.

▌ RIGHT
The Norman Cob has always been noted for its energetic action. The lively, free-moving trot is characteristic of the breed.

▌ BELOW
The Norman Cob has the same kindly expression as the English Cob after which it is named.

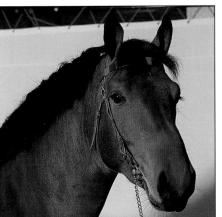

INTERESTING FACTS

The tail of the Norman Cob is still traditionally docked. Down the centuries this mutilation of horses' tails has been carried out for a variety of reasons: fashion, to prevent the tail becoming entangled with harness and equipment and, in ancient times, probably to serve some ritual purpose. It used to be the fashion to dock the tail of the English Cob, but the practice became illegal in Great Britain under the Docking and Nicking Act, 1948. Quite apart from the trauma of the operation, docking deprives the horse of a vital means of protection against flies.

BREED DESCRIPTION

Height 15.3 – 16.3hh.

Colour Chestnut, bay or bay-brown; occasionally red-roan or grey.

Conformation Overall strong, stocky build with short, well-proportioned limbs.

▌ LEFT
Strong and stockily built, the Norman Cob is a well-proportioned light draught horse. It lacks the massive proportions of the true heavy horse.

❙ BELOW LEFT
Small, strong and always grey, the Camargue has been an inspiration for artists and poets down the centuries.

❙ BELOW
The breed's ancient origins can be detected in the somewhat heavy, square head, which is reminiscent of that of the primitive horse.

Camargue

The tough little Camargue, the native horse of the inhospitable wastes of the Rhône delta in southern France, was not recognized as a breed until January 1968 yet it is almost certainly of ancient origin. It bears a strong resemblance to the horses depicted in the cave paintings of Lascaux, dating from 15,000 BC. Moreover, the even older horse skeletons unearthed at Solutré in south-east France in the nineteenth century could well be those of the breed's forebears.

During its long occupation of the marshlands, the indigenous horse must

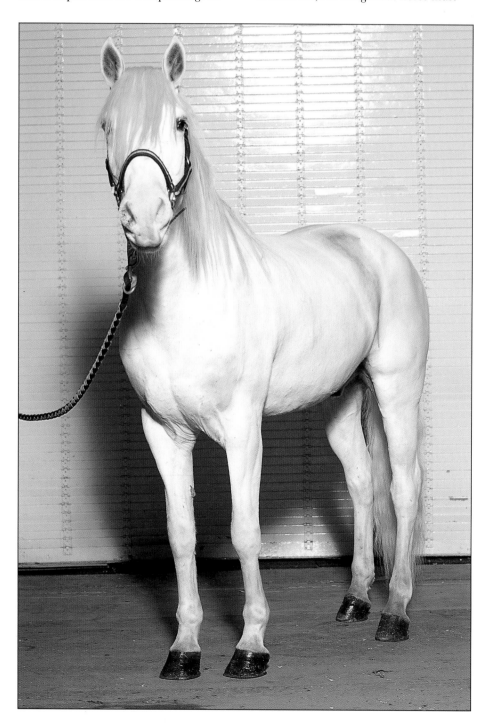

have been influenced by influxes of North African blood, but it has retained certain characteristics of the primitive horse, particularly in its rather heavy, square head.

The horses have always played an integral part in the everyday life of the Camargue, providing the guardians, or herdsmen, with strong, sure-footed mounts for their work with the herds of fighting bulls traditionally raised in the area. Despite its relatively small size, the Camargue horse has the strength and courage to carry a grown man safely over the most treacherous wetland terrain.

The herds, or *manades*, of Camargue horses, each with its own stallion, enjoy a semi-wild existence, being rounded up annually for inspection, branding of young stock, selection of suitable breeding stock and gelding of non-breeding males. Although the practice of fencing off pastureland and draining large areas for the cultivation of crops has, over the years, reduced the need for herdsmen, the horses are still very much a feature of the area. They have taken on a new role as mounts for the increasing number of tourists to the Camargue, which is famed for its wealth of wildlife.

BREED DESCRIPTION

Height 13.1 – 14.1hh.

Colour Grey.

Conformation Rather large, square head with short, wide-set ears; short neck; short, upright shoulders; fairly short back and deep chest; muscular hindquarters with short, sloping croup and long, bushy tail; strong, well-formed limbs with big knees and very hard, sound feet.

INTERESTING FACTS

The half-wild Camargue horses have long held a romantic fascination for artists and writers. In his poem "Horses on the Camargue", Roy Campbell penned these typically evocative lines:

...in a shroud of silence like the dead,
I heard a sudden harmony of hooves,
And, turning, saw afar
A hundred snowy horses unconfined,
The silver runaways of Neptune's car
Racing, spray-curled, like waves before
*   the wind.*
Sons of the Mistral, fleet
As him with whose strong gusts they love
*   to flee,*
Who shod the flying thunders of their feet
And plumed them with the snortings of
*   the sea.*

■ **BELOW LEFT**
Despite their semi-wild existence Camargue horses are perfectly amenable to training, as this French trick-riding expert demonstrates.

■ **BELOW**
The inhospitable wastes of the Rhône delta have produced a breed renowned for its toughness, strength and sure-footedness.

■ **BOTTOM**
Herding the fighting bulls reared in the region is the breed's traditional role. Despite its small size, the Camargue horse will carry a herdsman with great ease.

Ardennais

One of the world's premier heavy horses, the powerful but exceptionally docile Ardennais is of ancient origin and is named after its mountainous homeland region on the French–Belgian border.

The Ardennais used to be less massive – as late as the nineteenth century it was used not only for draught work but also for riding. Arab blood was introduced around 1810 and infusions of

BREED DESCRIPTION

Height 15 – 16hh.

Colour Roan, red-roan, iron grey, dark or liver chestnut and bay are the preferred colours. Bay-brown, light chestnut and palomino are admissible. Black, dappled grey and all other colours are inadmissible.

Conformation Straight profile with slightly prominent eye sockets, low, flat forehead, large expressive eyes, pricked ears and wide, open nostrils; medium-length neck, well set-on and generally arched; very strong shoulders; medium-heavy body with deep chest, rather short back and muscular loins; wide, rounded hindquarters; fairly short, strong and muscular limbs.

Thoroughbred, Percheron and Boulonnais were added later. These attempts to improve the breed were not a great success and were abandoned, but the Ardennais nevertheless continued to be a most useful animal. Its energy and stamina made it invaluable to the military during the Revolution, at the time of Empire and particularly during the ill-fated Russian campaign. During World

❙ BELOW
Massively built, but extremely docile, the bigger type of Ardennais makes the perfect partner for heavy agricultural work.

War I the Ardennais was in great demand as an artillery horse.

It was the requirements of agriculture and other heavy draught work which led to the development of a heavier stamp of horse and today, in addition to the original small Ardennais, two other types are recognized: a larger version of the Ardennais, known as the Auxois and the heavier, larger framed Ardennais du Nord (formerly known as the Trait du Nord), the result of using outcrosses to the Belgian Draught.

▌ ABOVE
The Ardennais can still be found working on the land. Its ability to thrive on a minimum of feed makes it an economical proposition for the farmers of small holdings.

▌ BELOW
Roan is a very typical coat colouring of the breed. The eyes are invariably large, with an intelligent, gentle expression.

INTERESTING FACTS

In their writings some 2,000 years ago both the Greek historian Herodotus and the Roman emperor Julius Caesar made particular mention of the horses of north-eastern France, then known as northern Gaul, extolling their stamina and toughness. Skeletons unearthed in the region suggest that these horses stood 15hh – the height of the smaller type of Ardennais still seen today. These were the ancestors of the modern Ardennais.

Selle Français

France has been well to the fore in the development of a modern sports horse, the Cheval de Selle Français (French Saddle Horse) being one of the great warmblood breeding success stories of the twentieth century. The term Selle Français came into use in December 1958 and the first stud book was published in 1965.

The French, with their great tradition of horse breeding, laid the foundations for their modern, quality riding horse as far back as the early nineteenth century, when many regions of the country began to import English Thoroughbred and half-

▌ ABOVE
A quality head, set on a long, elegant neck, is typical of the Selle Français. The breed is one of the world's most successful competition horses.

BREED DESCRIPTION

Height: Medium weight small, 15.3hh and under; medium, 15.3 – 16.1hh; large, over 16.1hh.

Height: Heavyweight small, under 16hh; large, 16hh and over. (The classification "medium" or "heavy" is based on the horse's weight-carrying ability, judged on conformation.)

Colour Predominantly chestnut, though all colours are permissible.

Conformation Refined head; long, elegant neck; sloping shoulders; strong body with well-sprung ribs; broad, powerful hindquarters; strong limbs with particularly powerful forearms, pronounced joints and good bone.

▌ RIGHT
English Thoroughbred and French Trotter blood provided the base for the Selle Français. Its harmonious proportions and overall appearance are very reminiscent of the Thoroughbred.

■ BELOW
Some Selle Français horses such as The Fellow (in the red colours) have the speed to take on, and beat, full Thoroughbreds on the racecourse.

■ BOTTOM LEFT
The breed excels at show jumping. This attractive bay mare, Miss, won team and individual silver medals at the 1994 World Equestrian Games.

INTERESTING FACTS

Although the most important influence on the Selle Français has undoubtedly been the Thoroughbred, the French Trotter has also been a factor, not least in the pedigrees of the famous show jumpers Galoubet and Jappeloup. Galoubet has trotter blood on his dam's side, albeit a couple of generations back. But the spring-heeled little Jappeloup, whose brilliant show-jumping career culminated with success in the individual championship at the 1988 Olympic Games in Seoul and a team gold medal in the 1990 World Equestrian Games, was actually by a trotter, Tyrol II, out of a Thoroughbred mare, Vénérable.

Interestingly, Jappeloup lacked the harmonious paces usually associated with the Selle Français. He was notoriously clumsy (many a human had their feet trodden on in his company) and a far from comfortable ride. This was almost certainly the result of his powerful hindquarters – he stood higher behind the saddle than in front, typical trotter conformation.

bred stallions to cross with their local, less refined, mares (the chief exceptions were the Limousin and south-west regions which specialized in breeding Anglo-Arabs). In Normandy, always a stronghold of horse breeding, two important horses evolved: a fast trotter, later to become the French Trotter (many of the half-breds imported from England came from Norfolk Roadster stock) and the Anglo-Norman. The vast majority of today's Selle Français horses trace back to the Anglo-Norman.

French Warmblood breeding differs from that in neighbouring countries, where the grading system is all-important. Success in competition by stallions, mares and their progeny or relatives forms the basis for selection in France. It is a system which, in a comparatively short space of time, has produced a highly successful competition horse, in appearance reminiscent of the Thoroughbred (which provided its most famous foundation sires) and possessing the necessary spirit to survive the cut and thrust of modern competitive sports. The Selle Français shines, above all, at show jumping where its claims to fame include Jappeloup (1987 European and 1988 Olympic Champion), Quito de Baussy (1990 World Champion), I Love You (1983 World Cup winner) and Galoubet (1982 world team gold medallist).

■ BELOW
Thanks to the Thoroughbred blood in their veins, Selle Français horses have the speed and stamina to succeed in three-day eventing.

French Trotter

France – the country with the greatest tradition of trotting racing outside the United States – developed its own strain of trotter by crossing English Thoroughbreds, half-breds and Norfolk Roadsters with robust Norman mares. The process began in the early nineteenth century. The first French trotting races, which were ridden, not driven, took place in 1806 on the Champ de Mars in Paris. As the sport began to increase in popularity, purpose-built race tracks were opened, the first being at Cherbourg in the 1830s, and the breed developed and improved. In 1861 an Imperial decree gave official encouragement to the sport, leading to the formation of its first governing body.

The Anglo-Norman developed into a fine trotter and five important bloodlines became established: Conquérant, Normand, Lavater, Phaeton and Fuchsia.

BREED DESCRIPTION

Height Average about 16.2hh. The larger horses tend to make the best ridden trotters.

Colour All colours admissible. Chestnut, bay and brown are predominant with some roan. Grey is rare.

Conformation Well-sloped shoulders, giving good ground-covering action; short, strong body; immensely powerful, often sloping, hindquarters.

▌ TOP RIGHT
The French Trotter has muc
about its general appearanc
sturdily built and rather less

▌ RIGHT
Racing under saddle, as well as in harness, has ensured the continued quality of this old-established breed, which has played an important part in the development of the Selle Français.

■ LEFT
French Trotters are
sometimes used in
the sport of skijoring,
in which the horse
pulls its human
partner on skis.

The premier driven trotting race in France is
the Prix d'Amérique. Its ridden equivalent is
the Prix de Cornulier. Both are run over
1 mile 5 furlongs (2,650m) at the leading
French track, the Hippodrome de Vincennes
which, with its downhill start and testing
uphill finish, is unique among raceways,
which are usually flat. The Prix d'Amérique is
the driven equivalent of flat racing's all-age
international championship of Europe, the
Prix de l'Arc de Triomphe. The Prix de
Cornulier is the world's richest ridden trotting
race. Very occasionally outstanding horses
appear which are equally brilliant in harness
and under saddle. Venutar, Masina, Tidalium
Pelo and Bellino II all share the distinction of
having won both the Prix d'Amérique and the
Prix de Cornulier.

Conquérant and Normand were both by
the English half-bred Young Rattler. This
son of the Thoroughbred Rattler is
sometimes called "the French Messenger"
(Messenger being the foundation sire of
the Standardbred) because of the
enormous influence he has had on trotter
breeding in France. Lavater was another
example of the English connection, being
by a Norfolk Roadster. The most
prepotent of all the early stallions was
Fuchsia. Foaled in 1883 he sired nearly
400 trotters and more than 100 of his sons
produced winners. Some Standardbred
blood was introduced over the years to
give the breed more speed but the
Trotteur Français Stud Book was closed to
non-French-bred horses in 1937 and has
only been opened a fraction in recent
years to allow a very limited number of
carefully selected French/Standardbred
crosses to be admitted.

The French have never totally given
up ridden racing. Some ten per cent of
today's trotting races staged in France are
under saddle and they have an important
effect on breeding. Because ridden
trotters race under comparatively heavy
weights they must accordingly be well built
horses with good balance and level action.
These quality horses have played a large
part in maintaining the overall standard of
the French Trotter.

■ ABOVE RIGHT
Powerful hindquarters
are typical of the
breed, the best
examples of which can
trot at speeds not
much less than those
of the galloping
Thoroughbred.

■ RIGHT
Specially designed
vehicles are used to
replace the bike-wheel
sulky for racing on
snow. Unlike pacers,
trotters always race
without hobbles on
their legs.

Percheron

The elegant, free-moving Percheron originated in La Perche, in the south of Normandy. Its ancestors were Arabian horses brought to Europe by the Moors. The oriental influence is believed to have begun following the defeat of the Moors by Charles Martel near Poitiers in AD 732, and was continued after the First Crusade in 1099, when Robert, Comte de Rotrou, imported more Arab horses into France. Much later, during the eighteenth century, Arab stallions at the Royal Stud at Le Pin were made available to breeders of Percherons to upgrade their stock. The

eastern influence continued until relatively recent times, one of the most important early Percheron stallions, Jean le Blanc (foaled in about 1830), being the son of the Arab stallion Gallipoly. The Percheron's great strength and courage, coupled with its sound limbs and

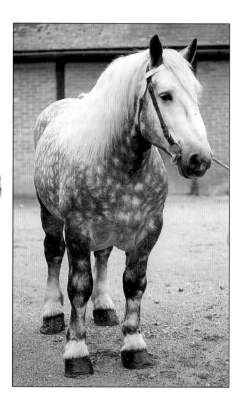

▌ LEFT
The Percheron has a fine head with prominent, alert eyes and wide, open nostrils.

▌ ABOVE RIGHT
The breed is noted for its broad, deep chest, powerful forearms and excellent feet.

▌ RIGHT
Well-proportioned and clean-limbed (that is, without feather on the lower legs), the Percheron is an elegant horse possessed of surprisingly free-moving paces considering its great size.

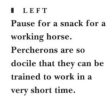
FAR LEFT
The quality and excellent movement of the modern Percheron reflect the Arab influence on the breed.

LEFT
Pause for a snack for a working horse. Percherons are so docile that they can be trained to work in a very short time.

BELOW
Thanks to its good action and amenable temperament, the Percheron goes equally well under saddle and in harness.

longevity, made it tremendously popular in various fields: as a war horse, as a carriage horse and on the land. For some four decades during the late nineteenth and early twentieth centuries it was in great demand world wide, both for work purposes and as an improver of other heavy breeds. French breeders exported a great number of Percherons, which proved to be the most adaptable of horses whatever the climate. Many went to England, some to Australia (the Percheron is said to be the first heavy horse to be taken there) and South America, and the breed became particularly popular in North America, where the black coat colouring was preferred to the grey. American buyers also favoured a heavyweight horse which, together with the need elsewhere for big horses to work on the railways, encouraged the breeding of more massive animals. Despite its great size, however, the modern Percheron is very much a quality animal, retaining the long, low action of its ancestors.

BREED DESCRIPTION

Height 15.2 – 17hh. Average 16.1hh.

Colour Grey or black.

Conformation Fine head, with broad, square forehead, fine, long ears, prominent, alert eyes, straight profile and flat nose with wide, open nostrils; long, arched neck with fairly thick mane; sloping shoulders with prominent withers; broad, deep chest with fairly prominent sternum, short, straight back and loins with great depth through the girth and well-sprung ribs; long, sloping hindquarters; clean, sound limbs with prominent, powerful forearms and long, muscular thighs, large knees and hocks, small, strong fetlock joints and good, strong feet.

Breton

Short-legged and heavily built, the Breton is a surprisingly active heavy horse, with an especially lively trot: characteristics that testify to its Norfolk Roadster and, even further back, Arab ancestry. Like so many southern European horse breeders, those in Brittany used horses brought back from the Middle East by the Crusaders to cross with their more plebeian native stock adding, in more recent times, infusions of blood from England and a number of continental countries – the latter not always with successful results.

Down the centuries there has always been more than one type of Breton horse. Two were identified in the Middle Ages, the Sommier and the Roussin. The Sommier was descended from stock bred mainly in the north of Brittany and was used for pack and agricultural work. The Roussin, a much lighter stamp of animal, was found in the south and some central parts of the region and was a popular

■ LEFT
Although the Breton is prized in the French meat trade, some examples of these attractive horses can still be seen at work as draught animals.

■ BELOW
Chestnut is the most usual colour for the Breton. The beautiful, kind eyes are set in a wide, somewhat square head.

saddle horse, noted for its comfortable, ambling gait.

Although the Breton is no longer thought of as a saddle horse, it does still come in different types – a large and small draught, and a coach-horse type known as the Postier, which is built on less massive lines than the draught horse. The Postier owes its lighter conformation and brilliant paces to infusions of Norfolk Roadster blood from England during the nineteenth century.

An early-maturing animal, the Breton is highly regarded in the French meat trade for the high yield and quality of meat it produces. However, it is still also valued as a draught animal and some Bretons can still be seen working on the land, particularly in the vineyards.

INTERESTING FACTS

The Breton is a hardy, adaptable animal and a most willing worker. Because of its ability to work in hot climates, it has been used for upgrading purposes by breeders in Italy, Spain and even as far afield as Japan.

BREED DESCRIPTION

Height 15 – 16.1hh.

Colour Mainly chestnut; some red roan, bay and grey; black rarely occurs.

Conformation Squarish head with straight profile, open nostrils, bright eyes and small, fairly low-set ears; short, strong and slightly arched neck; rather short but sloping shoulders; short, broad and strong body with well-sprung ribs; very powerful hindquarters; short, strong limbs with very muscular thighs and forearms.

■ RIGHT
Stocky and short-legged, the Breton is nevertheless a very active mover and has been used over the years as a warhorse, draught horse, pack-horse, coach horse – and even a riding horse.

Boulonnais

The gentle Boulonnais, the most elegant of all the heavy horse breeds, traces back to Roman times. It is a native of north-west France and, like the Percheron, was greatly influenced by oriental blood. The Arab influence occurred more than once. First there was the arrival of the Roman armies, with their horses of eastern origin, who massed on the French coast before invading Britain. Then there were the Crusaders, who brought more eastern horses back with them. Two great noblemen in particular, Robert, Comte d'Artois and Eustache, Comte de Boulogne, are credited with importing Arab horses for use in their stables at this time. There was a slight change of direction during the fourteenth century, when Mecklenburg blood from Germany was introduced in order to breed a sturdier animal capable of carrying knights with their new, plated armour.

The term Boulonnais dates from the seventeenth century and reflects the main breeding region of that name on the north French coast. Sadly, the number of Boulonnais horses was seriously depleted during World War I because their chief breeding grounds were right at the heart of the battle zone. World War II had a second serious impact on the breed just as it was recovering. These two setbacks, plus the rapid spread of mechanization following World War II all but signalled the death blow of this fine horse. Fortunately it did survive, thanks to the efforts of a few dedicated enthusiasts, and although the meat trade features as one of the prime outlets for breeders, some Boulonnais horses may still be seen working small farms, where they can prove more effective and economical than tractors. Despite its size and substantial build, it is still possible to detect traces of the breed's Arab ancestry both in the small, refined head, with its large, expressive eyes, and in its outgoing nature.

LEFT
Famous for its gentle nature, the Boulonnais is the most elegant of the heavy horse breeds.

BREED DESCRIPTION

Height 15.3 – 16.3hh.

Colour All shades of grey.

Conformation Elegant head, short and broad overall, with straight profile, wide forehead, slightly prominent eye sockets, strong, rounded, widely spaced jowls, large, bright eyes, small, erect ears, open nostrils and small mouth (in mares the head is slightly longer and less heavy); thick, often arched, neck with thick mane; muscular shoulders with fairly prominent withers; broad, straight back, broad chest and well-sprung ribs; round, muscular hindquarters with fairly high-set, thick tail; strong limbs with very prominent muscular projections in the forearms and thighs, short, thick cannons, large, flat joints and no feather.

INTERESTING FACTS

Two types of Boulonnais evolved: a large, heavy version for use in agriculture and industry, and a smaller, lighter horse suitable for less strenuous work on small-holdings and in light draught work. At one time the small type was known as the *maréeur* or *mareyeur* (fish merchant) because it was used for the transportation of fish from Boulogne to Paris. Nowadays the small type is used in agriculture, the meat trade favouring the larger animal.

BELOW
Boulonnais horses are branded with an anchor on the neck, reflecting their maritime homeland.

Trakehner

Of all the warmbloods, the Trakehner is the closest in appearance to the Thoroughbred. Organized breeding of this attractive riding horse began in 1732, when Friedrich Wilhelm I of Prussia established the Royal Trakehner Stud Administration in East Prussia (now part of Poland). A great deal of Thoroughbred and Arab blood was used to upgrade the local horses. These were descendants of the tough little Schweiken breed known to the Teutonic knights who colonized the region during the early thirteenth century. The Schweiken was a descendant of the

Konik pony, which traces back to the primitive Tarpan.

Towards the end of the eighteenth century a determined effort was made to improve the Trakehner, or East Prussian, as it was also known. Inferior breeding stock at the Royal Stud was drastically weeded out, a process which led to the swift development of the Trakehner. It was soon much in demand, first as a carriage horse and subsequently as an army remount.

Renowned for its twin qualities of elegance and toughness, the Trakehner flourished for nearly two centuries – until the disastrous upheaval of World War II. During the autumn and winter of 1944 the breed suffered catastrophic losses as desperate efforts were made to evacuate the horses before the arrival of the advancing Russian troops. Of the

thousands of Trakehners, many of them mares with foals at foot, who set off on the 900 mile (1,450km) journey west across Europe, few survived. Before their flight there were more than 25,000 horses registered in the East Prussian stud book. A mere 1,200 or so made it to the West

∎ ABOVE RIGHT
The Trakehner is noted for its refined head. Large eyes and a small, tapered muzzle enhance the overall impression of quality.

∎ RIGHT
The Trakehner's elegant outline owes much to the Thoroughbred influence. The Trakehner, in its turn, has been used in the development of the Dutch, Danish and Swedish Warmbloods.

BREED DESCRIPTION

Height Average 16 – 16.2hh.

Colour Any solid colour.

Conformation Refined head with large eyes and small muzzle; elegant, tapering neck; well-sloped shoulders; strong, medium-length body, well ribbed-up; well-rounded hindquarters; hard limbs with short cannons and excellent, sound feet.

INTERESTING FACTS

One of the most famous examples of the Trakehner is the show jumper Abdullah, a handsome grey stallion who competed for the United States. Ridden by Conrad Homfeld, he won a team gold medal and the individual silver at the 1984 Olympic Games and was victorious in the World Cup the following year. Abdullah was originally exported *in utero* to Canada and was foaled in 1970. After his retirement from competition he was used for breeding in many countries, thanks to the use of frozen semen.

■ **LEFT**
Like the Thoroughbred, the Trakehner is possessed of courage and stamina, qualities which make it suitable for tough sports such as carriage driving.

■ **BELOW LEFT**
The powers of endurance which helped the breed survive the harsh times of World War II stand the breed in good stead in the modern sport of eventing.

■ **BELOW**
The show-jumping stallion Abdullah demonstrated the breed's fine qualities to great advantage when winning a team gold medal at the 1984 Olympic Games.

and many of these failed to survive in the very harsh economic conditions of post-war Germany.

Incredibly, thanks to the dedicated efforts of the keepers of the original stud book, the Trakehner did not die out. The surviving equine evacuees were tracked down and re-registered in West Germany and, as breeding resumed and numbers increased, the Trakehner began to take its place in the modern equestrian world. Valued for its good conformation and action, its spirited temperament and its endurance, it has found favour both as a competition horse and as an improver of other warmbloods.

Hanoverian

George II, Elector of Hanover and King of England, was instrumental in the establishment of this famous German warmblood, thanks to the foundation of the state stud at Celle in 1735. The aim was to provide local people with the services of good quality stallions at nominal fees, the original horses being Holsteins of predominantly Andalusian and Neapolitan blood. Thanks to the later

▮ LEFT
Previously bred as an all-purpose work horse, the modern Hanoverian has been refined for use in equestrian sports.

BREED DESCRIPTION

Height 15.3 – 16.2hh.

Colour All solid colours.

Conformation Medium-sized head, clean cut and expressive, with large, lively eyes and good free cheek bones; long, fine neck; large, sloping shoulders with pronounced withers; strong, deep body; muscular hindquarters with well set-on tail; well-muscled limbs with large, pronounced joints and well-formed, hard hooves.

▮ ABOVE RIGHT
Thoroughbreds and Trakehners were used in the development of the present-day Hanoverian. Their influence can be seen in the breed's clean-cut head.

▮ RIGHT
The Hanoverian is noted more for its strength than its speed, hence the many successes of its representatives in dressage and show jumping.

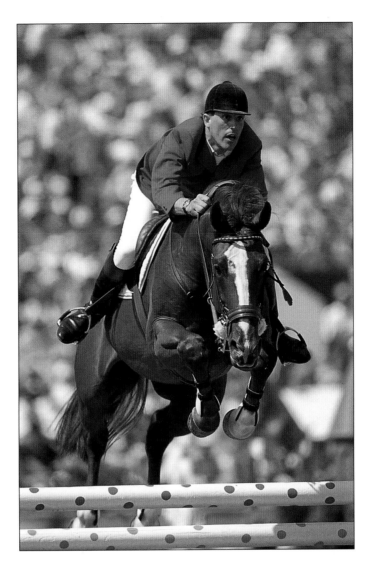

▌ LEFT
Hanoverians have found favour throughout the world as show jumpers. Amadeus Z, bred in Belgium, is seen competing for Holland at the 1994 World Equestrian Games.

importation of English horses, including Thoroughbreds, the Hanoverian gradually began to show more quality, the aim being to produce a good all-purpose animal that was capable of working on the land but also suitable for ridden work and for use as a light carriage horse.

In common with so many other horse-breeding enterprises, the development of the Hanoverian at Celle was adversely affected by war. By the end of the eighteenth century the stud had over 100 stallions, but by 1816, after the Napoleonic wars, a mere thirty remained. To help make up for these losses, more outside blood was brought in, especially Thoroughbred. But the time came when the breed was tending to become too light for the work required of it and this influence was accordingly reduced.

After World War II, however, the Hanoverian had to be adapted to a new way of life if the breed was to survive and Thoroughbred blood was again introduced, along with Trakehner, to produce a warmblood suited to the demands of the leisure-horse market.

The modern Hanoverian is lighter and less coarse than of old and is noted for its good, honest temperament. In common with other German warmbloods, stallions are only licensed if they pass the required veterinary inspection and, after licensing, must pass ridden performance tests. Hanoverians are among the world's most sought-after sports horses, their strength and athleticism making them especially suitable for dressage and show jumping.

▌ LEFT
Dressage is the other sport at which the Hanoverian excels. With its great strength and true, energetic action, it is well suited to this demanding discipline.

Holstein

The Holstein is probably the oldest of the German warmbloods, dating back several centuries. As early as the seventeenth century horses bred in the region were much in demand in France, Denmark and Italy. The old Holstein horses contained mixed blood, including German, Neapolitan, Spanish and oriental. During the nineteenth century they were crossed with Yorkshire Coach Horses, a policy which helped give the breed a distinctive high knee action, great presence and an exceptionally tractable nature. Holsteins became renowned for being tough but handsome carriage horses and subsequently as army remounts.

The Traventhall Stud, founded by the Prussians in 1867 in Schleswig-Holstein, is considered the modern Holstein's birthplace. However, this stud is no longer in operation and the breeds main base is now at Elmshorn.

To produce a stamp of horse suitable for today's requirements, some Thoroughbred blood was used in the period after World War II, which resulted in a lighter type of horse with less high, "carriage-horse" action and a better shoulder. Although the infusions of Thoroughbred blood may have made the Holstein rather more excitable than it was

■ ABOVE
This handsome head, with its alert, intelligent expression, is typical of the Holstein.

■ LEFT
Formerly bred for use as a carriage horse and army remount, the Holstein was upgraded into a better-quality animal through the introduction of a certain amount of Thoroughbred blood.

One of the most celebrated Holstein horses of all time was the big bay gelding Meteor, the only show jumper to have won a medal at three Olympic Games. Foaled in 1943, he won the individual bronze medal at the 1952 Games and four years later helped Germany win the team gold in Stockholm, where he finished fourth individually. In Rome in 1960, at the age of 17, he won a second team gold medal and finished sixth in the individual contest. Ridden by Fritz Thiedemann, an exceptionally talented all-round horseman, Meteor was an outstanding ambassador for the Holstein breed. He died in 1966 and is buried at Elmshorn, the breed's headquarters.

■ **FAR LEFT**
Show jumping is a sport at which the Holstein, with its intelligent and bold character, has excelled for many years.

■ **BELOW**
The breed is noted for its powerful action, which is used to good effect in Grand Prix dressage.

of old, it has, generally speaking, retained its good temperament. Its intelligence and boldness make it a first-rate mount for top-level dressage and show jumping.

Holstein horses are not bred in such quantity as some other warmbloods nor is their breeding area particularly large. Possibly as a result, there is less variation in overall type.

■ **BELOW**
Originally prized as tough, active carriage horses, Holsteins can still be seen in harness in the competitive discipline of four-in-hand driving.

BREED DESCRIPTION

Height Approximately 16 – 17hh.

Colour All colours permissible. Bay with black points and brown predominate. Grey is quite common, chestnut less so.

Conformation Expressive head, well set-on and in proportion to the size of the horse, with big, bright eyes; long, muscular and slightly arched neck; long, sloping shoulders; strong back, deep, wide chest and muscular loins; strong, muscular hindquarters with well-muscled thighs, stifles and gaskins; short, strong cannon bones, flat knees, big, clean hocks, medium-length pasterns and good, hard feet.

Oldenburg

The Oldenburg, Germany's heaviest type of warmblood, was originally developed as a coach horse and was based on the old Friesian horses bred in the region between the River Weser and the Netherlands. The breed takes its name from Count Anton Gunther von Oldenburg (1603–67), who played a leading part in its development, crossing stallions from Italy and Spain with the native stock. Later breeders introduced Thoroughbred, Cleveland Bay, Hanoverian and Norman blood. The result was a big upstanding horse, measuring a good 17hh, and fairly heavily built. Unlike most large animals, however, it matured early which undoubtedly popularized it as a work horse.

▌ LEFT
The Oldenburg was originally bred as a coach horse. It is the heaviest of the German Warmbloods.

BREED DESCRIPTION

Height Approximately 16 – 17hh.

Colour Predominantly brown, black and bay.

Conformation Rather plain head, occasionally with a Roman nose; fairly long, very strong neck; sloping, muscular shoulders; powerfully built body with deep chest; strong hindquarters with high-set tail; fairly short limbs with large joints and plenty of bone.

▌ LEFT
Careful breeding has helped eradicate coach-horse characteristics such as upright shoulders and a long back, though some modern Oldenburgs retain the rather high knee action of their forebears.

▎ LEFT
The German rider Franke Sloothaak on his way to becoming World Show Jumping Champion in 1994. His mount is the Oldenburg mare, Weihaiwej.

As coach horses gave way to motorized transport in the early twentieth century, breeders had of necessity to change the type of the Oldenburg and look more to the production of a general-purpose farm horse. More recently, further infusions of Thoroughbred blood, and some Selle Français, have produced a horse which is considerably finer than its coaching ancestors and well able to hold its own in the competitive sports, working equally well under saddle or in harness. The Oldenburg still tends to be a big individual compared with other warmbloods but many of the coach-horse characteristics, such as an upright shoulder and long back, have been eliminated. The knee action still tends to be a little on the high side.

Oldenburg horses are exported to many countries and have proved particularly popular in the United States.

▎ BELOW
From coach horse to dressage horse: refinement of the breed has been brought about through the introduction of Thoroughbred and Selle Français blood, making the present-day Oldenburg an outstanding sports horse.

INTERESTING FACTS

Olympic Bonfire, an Oldenburg gelding foaled in 1983, won the World Dressage Freestyle to Music Championship in 1994 when ridden by the leading Dutch rider, Anky van Grunsven.

Westphalian

Closely related to the Hanoverian, the Westphalian is bred in the region of Nordrhein-Westfalen, in the north-west of Germany. Its main breeding centre, Warendorf, is famous for being the home of German equestrianism (the National Federation is based there). The area has a long tradition of horse breeding. It is known that in the early nineteenth century East Prussian stallions were made available to local mare owners to enable them to upgrade their stock. Over the years various outcrosses were made, involving Oldenburg, Hanoverian, Friesian, Anglo-Norman and trotter blood and it was not until this century that breeders finally settled for just one influence: the Hanoverian. Today's Westphalian shares the bloodlines of the present-day Hanoverian, although there are also several important ones which have developed specifically in the Westphalia region.

> **BREED DESCRIPTION**
>
> **Height** 15.3 – 16.2hh.
>
> **Colour** All solid colours.
>
> **Conformation** Intelligent head with good width between the eyes; well-shaped neck; deep, broad body; powerful hindquarters, although they can be a little flat.

▮ **ABOVE**
The Westphalian has the same clean-cut good looks as the Hanoverian, with whom it shares a common ancestry.

▮ **RIGHT**
The conformation is typical of that of the modern sports horse: a good length of neck, deep body and powerful hindquarters. It tends to be a little longer in the leg than the Hanoverian.

INTERESTING FACTS

Famous Westphalian horses include Rembrandt (Olympic dressage champion in 1988 and 1992, ridden by Nicole Uphoff-Becker); Ahlerich (Olympic dressage champion in 1984, ridden by Reiner Klimke); Fire (winner of the World Show Jumping Championship in 1982, ridden by Norbert Koof) and Roman (winner of the World Show Jumping Championship in 1978, ridden by Gerd Wiltfang). Rembrandt, one of the most handsome representatives of the breed, was the first horse in the history of the Olympic Games to win two individual gold medals for dressage. He was European champion in 1989 and also took the individual title at the first World Equestrian Games, held in Stockholm in 1990.

▌ ABOVE RIGHT
Two Step is a Westphalian who has found fame as a show jumper. Originally named Polydektes, he is by Polydor, one of the breed's most successful sires of competition horses.

▌ RIGHT
Ahlerich was one of the breed's most outstanding performers in the world of dressage. He crowned a gloriously successful Grand Prix career with victory at the 1984 Olympic Games in Los Angeles.

■ BELOW
The head is rather plain but the expression is
kindly.

■ BOTTOM
The Schleswig is generally chestnut in colour.

Schleswig

A sturdy, compact heavy horse, the
Schleswig comes from the northernmost
region of Germany, Schleswig-Holstein,
which borders on to Denmark and which
was, indeed, at various times actually part
of that country. It is not surprising, therefore, that the Schleswig bears a marked
resemblance to the Jutland, the Danish
heavy breed to which it is closely related.
The Schleswig was developed during the
second half of the nineteenth century as a
medium-sized draught horse. Infusions of
lighter blood, including Yorkshire Coach
Horse and Thoroughbred, were made
towards the end of the century but these
had no lasting effect on the breed. Popular as a tram and bus horse, and for use on
the land and in forestry, the breed survived World War I (during which its
homeland was under Danish rule) although
it was seriously depleted in both numbers
and quality. The subsequent introduction
of Breton and Boulonnais blood from

■ BELOW
The head is rather plain but the expression is
kindly.

■ BOTTOM
The Schleswig is generally chestnut in colour.

France proved highly successful. The
Schleswig recovered and flourished in
large numbers until the years immediately
following World War II. In time, however,
mechanization took its usual toll, and
numbers dwindled drastically. In recent
years some of the surviving Schleswigs have
been bred back to Jutlands, in order to
increase the breed's size.

The attractive Schleswig horse, which often
has a flaxen mane and tail, is extremely
powerfully built and weighs in the region of
1,766lb (800kg).

South German

This strong and agile heavy horse is descended from the Austrian Noriker, which was introduced into Bavaria, in southern Germany, towards the end of the nineteenth century. With a view to improving and developing their own stamp of horse, breeders in Upper Bavaria added some Holstein and Oldenburg blood, while those in Lower Bavaria experimented with an extraordinary variety of outcrosses, from Oldenburg and Cleveland Bay to Clydesdale and Belgian Draught. In time, however, German breeders reverted to using the original Noriker blood for upgrading purposes. Originally called the Pinzgauer Noriker, after the region in Salzburg province from which that particular strain of the Austrian heavy horse came, the German version of the breed became known as the South German Heavy Horse. Today it is bred mainly in Bavaria and Baden Wurtemburg. It still resembles the Noriker, although it is inclined to stand a little less tall. It is a

well-proportioned horse, with a calm, docile temperament, and can be seen in parades and at shows as well as, occasionally, at work in agriculture.

▌ BELOW
The South German Coldblood has a large head and, typically, a docile expression.

▌ BOTTOM
The South German resembles the Noriker but is a little smaller.

The South German heavy horse is a popular attraction at shows. As well as being used by trick riders, it takes part in races – which it clearly enjoys!

BREED DESCRIPTION

Height Around 15.3hh.

Colour Brown, bay and chestnut.

Conformation Rather large head, with kind eye; short, strong neck; powerful shoulders; strong back with deep girth; good limbs with a little feather.

Cleveland Bay

A race of bay-coloured horses was being bred, primarily for pack work, in the north east of England as far back as mediaeval times. It was the preferred means of transport of the chapmen, or travelling salesmen of the day, and was accordingly known as the Chapman Horse. Taking the Chapman Horse as their base, seventeenth-century breeders used some of the Andalusian and Barb stallions that were being brought into the country at that time to produce a fine coach horse, renowned for its active paces and great stamina. This became known as the Cleveland Bay after the area where it

was chiefly bred. As roads improved, and a faster type of coach horse became necessary, some Thoroughbred blood was introduced, usually by means of putting half-bred stallions to Cleveland mares. This lighter, faster version of the

Cleveland Bay was called the Yorkshire Coach Horse. It had its own breed society, founded in 1886, and stud book. But the coming of motorized transport signalled the demise of coach horses everywhere and the Yorkshire breed was no exception.

▌ ABOVE
The Cleveland Bay is the descendant of a race of bay-coloured horses bred in north-eastern England since medieval times.

▌ LEFT
A handsome, upstanding stamp of horse, the Cleveland Bay produces excellent hunters when crossed with the Thoroughbred.

LEFT AND FAR LEFT
Cleveland Bay horses at the Royal Mews in London testify to the interest taken in the preservation of this historic breed by Queen Elizabeth II.

Its stud book was finally closed in 1936, by which time the breed had virtually died out. Fortunately the Cleveland Bay survived, albeit in small numbers. Crossed with the Thoroughbred, the breed produces fine upstanding heavyweight hunters and excellent carriage horses. The Cleveland Bay has a true, straight and free action (high action is not characteristic of the breed), moves freely from the shoulder and covers the ground well. As well as making an excellent hunter and carriage horse, the Cleveland Bay, when crossed with the Thoroughbred, has also produced some first-rate show jumpers.

BREED DESCRIPTION

Height 16 – 16.2hh, though height does not disqualify an otherwise good animal.

Colour Bay with black points.

Conformation Bold head, not too small, with large, well-set, kind eyes and large, fine ears; long, lean neck; deep, sloping, muscular shoulders; deep, wide body, with muscular loins, powerful hindquarters and well set-on tail; clean limbs (without feather), with muscular forearms, thighs and second thighs, large knees and hocks, and strong, sloping pasterns; good, sound feet.

INTERESTING FACTS

The survival of the Cleveland Bay was aided in no small measure by Queen Elizabeth II. A colt named Mulgrave Supreme, due to be sent to the United States, was bought by the Queen, subsequently broken to saddle and to harness and then made available to breeders of Cleveland Bays, both pure- and part-bred, throughout Britain. This tremendously successful promotional exercise sparked off renewed enthusiasm among breeders. Prince Philip further enhanced the breed's profile by driving, for many years, teams of pure- and part-bred Cleveland Bays at international level.

RIGHT
For many years HRH The Duke of Edinburgh drove a team of Cleveland Bays in international four-in-hand events. They have excellent ground-covering action, well suited to work both in harness and under saddle.

Hackney

The Hackney, with its high-stepping action, is a native of England though it is prized the world over as a carriage horse, especially in the show ring. The Hackney horse originated in the late seventeenth and early eighteenth centuries and is a descendant of the famous English trotting horses of the time, the Yorkshire Trotter and the Norfolk Roadster. These horses had a common ancestor, a horse known as the Original Shales, who was foaled in 1755 and was by the Thoroughbred Blaze out of a mare described as a "hackney". Blaze was by Flying Childers, generally recognized as being the first great racehorse. Blaze and his progeny, notably his two sons, Driver and Scot Shales, had a considerable influence on the development of the trotters of eastern England. Despite their shared ancestry,

do not use these Straps

the horses bred in Yorkshire and Norfolk developed somewhat different characteristics – those of Yorkshire origin tended to have more quality than those from Norfolk, which were more cob-like in appearance – but these regional

INTERESTING FACTS

The derivation of the word hackney is doubtful but it is thought to come from the Old French *haquenée*, "an ambling horse or mare, especially for ladies to ride on", and may be related to the Old Spanish and Portuguese *facanea* and Spanish *hacanea*. In the fourteenth century the word was latinized in England as *hakeneius*.

LEFT
Hackneys are popular in show rings throughout the world. Here they are being driven in an unusual three-horse combination known as a unicorn, comprising two wheelers and a leader.

distinctions later disappeared.

The Hackney pony was developed during the second half of the eighteenth century – earlier use of the term "Hackney ponies" almost certainly referred to small part-bred Hackney horses. It was the very enterprising Westmorland breeder, Christopher Wyndham Wilson, a remarkable man whose achievements included inventing the silo to store winter feed for farm animals, who was largely

responsible for the development of the true Hackney pony. Wilson used a variety of pony breeds, especially the Fell, as his foundation mares, crossing them with a good-looking Hackney horse named Sir George, who was sired in 1866 and stood less than 14hh. His policy of inbreeding to the prepotent Sir George enabled Wilson to achieve his aim of developing a Hackney with real pony characteristics and in due course other breeders followed his

lead. The original height limit for ponies, as recommended by the Hackney Horse Society, was 14.2hh but this was subsequently reduced to 14hh. The high-stepping action for which the Hackney is renowned was not developed until the second half of the nineteenth century, when it became the fashion to drive elegant, showy carriage horses. It is partly inherited, partly taught and can be enhanced by training.

RIGHT
In classes for single turnouts the Hackney is harnessed to a lightweight vehicle with pneumatic tyres.

OPPOSITE
The Hackney has a compact body, powerful shoulders and a deep chest. The limbs are strong and the feet invariably well formed.

horses necks shouldn't bend this way

Shire

England's most magnificent looking heavy horse is descended from the mediaeval warhorse known as the Great Horse, which was later given the name of the English Black. It was developed by crossing imported Flanders and Friesian horses with native stock to produce first a military mount and subsequently a farm and general draught horse. The introduction of the term "blacks" for these heavy horses is attributed to Oliver Cromwell, and was probably used originally to describe the imported Friesians, which are always black in colour. The main breeding areas of the

BREED DESCRIPTION

Height Stallions 16.2 – 17.2hh. Mares 16 – 17hh.

Colour Black, brown, bay or grey.

Conformation Lean head (neither too large nor too small), wide between the eyes, slightly Roman nose, large, prominent eyes with docile expression, and long, lean, sharp, sensitive ears; fairly long, slightly arched neck; deep, oblique shoulders, wide enough to support a collar; short, strong, muscular back, broad chest and wide, sweeping, muscular hindquarters with well let-down thighs; clean, hard limbs with 11–12 inches (28–30cm) of bone and broad, deep, flat hocks, set at the correct angle for leverage; fine, straight, silky feather; deep, solid feet with thick walls and open coronets.

▪ ABOVE RIGHT
The Roman nose, long, sharp ears, large eyes and docile expression are typical of the Shire, the archetypal "gentle giant".

▪ RIGHT
The magnificent Shire is descended from the medieval warhorse known as the Great Horse. It weighs in excess of 20cwt (1,016kg).

■ RIGHT
A team of twenty Shires makes a magnificent sight at an English horse show, admirably displaying the breed's tractable nature.

■ BELOW
A foal dozes in the summer sun. While Shires will never be seen in the same numbers as in olden times, the breed has enough enthusiasts to ensure its future.

INTERESTING FACTS

One of the earliest records of a Shire stallion standing at stud is of the horse known as the Packington Blind Horse. He was named after the village of Packington, near Ashby-de-la-Zouche, where he lived between 1755 and 1770. This horse, and horses said to be his progeny, had a significant influence on the breed during its formative years.

English Black were the Fen country and the Midland shires of Leicestershire, Lincolnshire, Derbyshire and Staffordshire, from which the breed eventually took its name. In the early days the breed displayed regional variations, horses bred in the Fens tending to be bigger, heavier and somewhat coarser than those from the "Shires". Those from Derbyshire and Leicestershire were predominantly black, while Staffordshire horses were more often brown.

It was not until the late nineteenth century that the breeding of these horses became formalized, as a result of the publication of the first stud book. In 1878 a breed society was set up under the title of the Old English Cart Horse Society. The name was changed in 1884 to the Shire Horse Society and the breed has been known as the Shire ever since.

Following the formation of the breed society, the Shire went from strength to strength, competing with great success in the leading agricultural shows of the time and attracting the interest of foreign buyers. Shire horses were soon being exported as far afield as North and South America, Russia and Australia. They also became an indispensable part of daily life in Britain. With their qualities of strength, stamina, soundness and good temperament, these gentle giants could be seen ploughing the land, hauling timber and pulling farm wagons, railway vans, brewers' drays and coal carts. Although mechanization took its customary toll, a Shire "revival" began in the 1960s and today these wonderful horses can again be seen at shows, ploughing the land and, not least, pulling brewers' drays on short-haul routes in cities.

■ LEFT AND ABOVE
Shires hitched to brewers' drays are a popular sight at many British horse and agricultural shows. Some are still used for short-haul work in inner cities, where they are more economical than motorized transport.

Suffolk

Britain's oldest heavy breed, the Suffolk or Suffolk Punch, is named after the East Anglian county where it has been bred since the sixteenth century. Little is known of its origins, but as far back as 1506 there is an historical reference to a distinctive type of Suffolk horse. The Suffolk was developed as a farm horse and with its tremendously strong shoulders and clean legs (i.e. free of feather) it is ideally suited to working on the very heavy clay soils of East Anglia.

The breed is unique in that all Suffolks trace back to a single stallion, known as Crisp's Horse of Ufford, foaled in 1760.

This mare shows the typical broad forehead and full, bright eyes of the Suffolk. All Suffolks are chestnut in colour – traditionally spelt without the middle "t".

Although there is plenty of width between the forelegs, the hindfeet are set close together. Such conformation prevents the horse damaging crops when working in the fields.

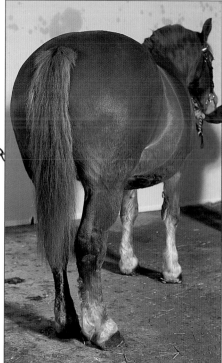

This purity is manifested in the fact that it always breeds true to colour: all Suffolks are "chesnut" (traditionally spelt without the first "t"). Quite apart from its coat colour, the Suffolk is quite unmistakable in appearance, having a heavy body set on comparatively short legs.

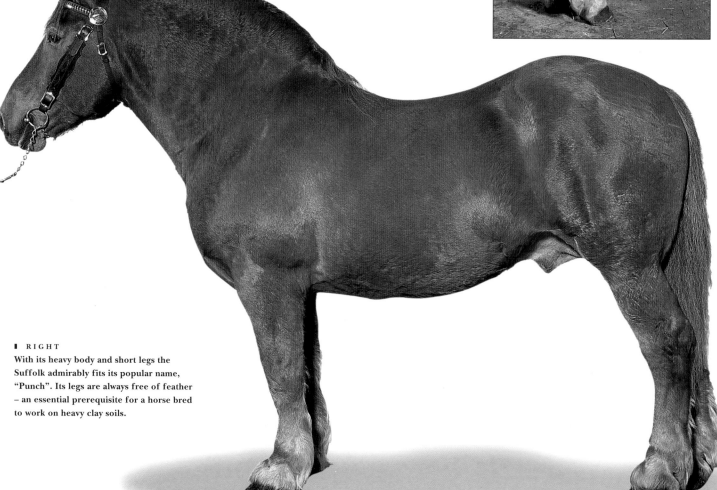

With its heavy body and short legs the Suffolk admirably fits its popular name, "Punch". Its legs are always free of feather – an essential prerequisite for a horse bred to work on heavy clay soils.

BREED DESCRIPTION

Height 16 – 16.3hh.

Colour Always "chesnut", of which seven shades are recognized, ranging from a pale mealy tone to a very dark, almost brown, shade. The most common is a bright reddish shade. A little white may occur on the face and the mane and tail are sometimes pale in colour.

Conformation Quite large head, with broad forehead; deep, tapering neck; long, muscular shoulders; deep, well-rounded body with strong quarters and well-set tail; fairly short, straight limbs with plenty of bone, sloping pasterns and no coarse hair; hard, sound, medium-sized feet.

INTERESTING FACTS

The ability of the Suffolk to thrive on less rations than other working heavy horses is well illustrated by the experiences of one farmer who, during the early part of this century, compared the feed requirements of two dozen cross-bred farm horses which he used for several years on one farm, and those of twenty-five Suffolks which he used for a similar period on another. While all the horses ate the same quantities of bulk food – hay, mangolds and chaff – the cross-breds each required 75lb (34kg) of corn per week, increasing by some 14–21lbs (6.4-9.5kg) per week as they grew older, while the Suffolks, even the older ones, kept their condition on a regular 50lb (22.7kg) per week.

Despite its size the Suffolk is a remarkably economical horse to keep, thriving and working on comparatively small rations. It matures early – Suffolks can be put to light work at two years of age and go into full work at three. It has an exceptionally amenable temperament and it is noted for its great soundness and longevity – it is common for horses to be in use and mares to be producing foals into their late teens and Suffolks often live until they are nearly thirty. The Suffolk's remarkable qualities combined to make it one of the most popular agricultural and draught horses of all time and, not surprisingly, its popularity spread abroad. There have been Suffolks in the United States for many years and representatives of the breed have also been exported to Australia, Africa, Russia and Pakistan (where they were used to produce army horses). Like the Shire, the Suffolk survived the coming of mechanization and can still be seen occasionally working the land, pulling drays and at shows, principally in eastern England.

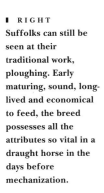

■ **ABOVE RIGHT**
A pair of present-day Suffolks drawing a vehicle of yesteryear.

■ **RIGHT**
Suffolks can still be seen at their traditional work, ploughing. Early maturing, sound, long-lived and economical to feed, the breed possesses all the attributes so vital in a draught horse in the days before mechanization.

Clydesdale

Scotland's breed of heavy horse, as its
name suggests, originated in that area of
Lanarkshire through which the Clyde river
runs. Today's Clydesdale, which developed
more recently than the other British heavy
breeds, began to evolve during the second
half of the eighteenth century when
imported Flemish stallions were used to
improve the stock, descended from pack
animals, of local farmers. Before that,
during the early part of the century, a
breeder named Paterson of Lochlyoch
had begun to produce horses which, by all
accounts, bore a distinct resemblance to
the modern Clydesdale, certainly as far as
colour was concerned. The stallion
Glancer, to whom many Clydesdales can
be traced back, was out of a mare known
as Lampit's Mare, who was believed to be a

BREED DESCRIPTION

Height Stallions 17.1 – 18hh. Mares
16.3 – 17.2hh

Colour Bay, brown or black. Chestnut is
rare. Often with a good deal of white on the
face and legs, which may run up on to the
body, particularly as flashes on the stomach.

Conformation Strong, intelligent head, with
broad forehead, wide muzzle, large nostrils,
bright, clear eyes and big ears; long, well-
arched neck; sloping shoulders with high
withers; short back with well-sprung ribs and
muscular hindquarters; straight limbs with
forelegs set well under the shoulders, long
pasterns and a fair amount of fine feather;
round, open feet.

▌ OPPOSITE PAGE
The brisk, ground-covering paces of the Clydesdale
make it eminently suitable for both agricultural and
heavy haulage work.

▌ ABOVE
Large, kind eyes and
big ears give these
Clydesdales the gentle,
sensible expression
typical of the breed.
Unlike the Shire, the
Clydesdale never has a
Roman nose.

▌ LEFT
Although the
Clydesdale is closely
related to the Shire,
it has a number of
distinguishing
features, the most
readily discernible
of which is the large
amount of white often
seen on the limbs and
extending up to the
lower parts of
the body.

I BELOW
Wearing traditional Scottish harness decorations, the Clydesdale makes a fine sight in the show ring.

INTERESTING FACTS

One of the most famous and influential stallions in the development of the Clydesdale was a dark brown horse named Prince of Wales, foaled in Ayrshire in 1866. He was a mixture of English and Scottish blood and had outstanding action. His stud fee of £40, by no means a small sum for those days, was well worth paying – young horses sired by him fetched anywhere from £2,000 to £3,000.

descendant of the Lochlyoch horses.

Shire blood was used in the breed's development – indeed the two leading Clydesdale breeders during the second half of the nineteenth century, Lawrence Drew and David Riddell, believed the Clydesdale and the Shire to be of the same origin, and regularly interbred the two.

The Clydesdale Horse Society was formed in 1877 and the first stud book was published the following year. By this time interest in the breed had spread to other countries and Clydesdales were soon

being exported, often in large numbers, to work the vast wheatlands of North America; others went to Australia, South America and Russia. It was, without doubt, the Clydesdale's docile nature combined with elegance and great activity that endeared it to heavy horse enthusiasts all over the world. Describing his action, the breed society says that the inside of every shoe should be made visible to anyone walking behind. The Clydesdale is an exceptionally sound horse, great emphasis having always been placed on good limbs and feet.

I RIGHT
Many Clydesdales were exported to North America to work in agriculture. Their descendants can still be seen, though in rather different roles. This team is being used to haul the starting stalls at Santa Anita Racetrack.

Furioso

Hungary has long enjoyed a world-wide reputation as a horse-breeding country and as a producer of fine horsemen. The famous stud farm at Mezöhegyes, founded in 1784 by the Emperor Josef II, quickly became established as one of the great breeding centres of Europe. One of the most important breeds developed there was the Furioso, which was produced by crossing Thoroughbreds with mainly Hungarian mares. The chief influences were the English Thoroughbred stallion, Furioso, after whom the breed was named and who was acquired by Mezöhegyes in 1841, and another English horse, North Star, who was imported during the 1850s. Using these two bloodlines Mezöhegyes began producing quality carriage horses and good, heavyweight riding horses. For a time these two bloodlines were kept separate, with North Star proving a particularly successful sire of harness racehorses. He was descended from the 1793 Derby winner, Waxy (a grandson of the great Eclipse), and is said to trace back to Norfolk Roadster blood, which could account for his progeny's success in harness. Towards the end of the nineteenth century the North Star and Furioso strains were merged, after which the Furioso became the dominant force.

BREED DESCRIPTION

Height About 16hh.

Colour Any solid colour.

Conformation Fine head (denoting its Thoroughbred ancestry); well-sloped shoulders; strong back; good strong limbs and feet.

INTERESTING FACTS

The Csikos horse herders of Hungary are renowned for their trick-riding skills. Their breathtaking displays, often performed with Furioso horses, are famous all over the world.

■ TOP
The present-day Furioso is a quality all-purpose riding horse, built on somewhat heavier lines than its Thoroughbred ancestors.

■ LEFT
Large herds of horses, including the Furioso, have traditionally been raised on the grasslands of Hungary.

Nonius

Like the Furioso, the more heavily built Nonius evolved at the Mezőhegyes stud farm founded by the Emperor Josef II. The breed's foundation sire was an Anglo-Norman horse by the name of Nonius Senior. He was foaled in 1810, captured in

BREED DESCRIPTION

Height Large type 15.3 – 16.2hh. Small type 14.3 – 15.3hh.

Colour Predominantly bay, with some black, brown and chestnut.

Conformation Attractive, honest head; sloping shoulders; broad, strong back; strong hindquarters; sound limbs.

France by the Austrians in 1814 and installed at Mezőhegyes in 1816. Nonius was said to be by a half-bred English stallion out of a Norman mare and almost certainly had Norfolk Roadster blood in him. He was by all accounts not the most prepossessing individual and would have won no prizes for conformation, but during his sixteen years at stud he became a tremendously successful sire. Mated with mares of various breeds, including Arab, Lipizzaner, Spanish and Turkish, as well as Hungarian, he produced good quality horses, the best of which were mated back to him. In this way a distinctive type emerged – to be known as the Nonius.

During the 1860s, infusions of Thoroughbred blood were made, a policy which led to the development of two different types of Nonius: one, a large horse suited to light agricultural work and as a carriage horse, the other, a smaller, finer animal suitable for riding. In more recent times, as the need for farm horses diminished, the larger type of Nonius was used mainly for driving, a skill at which Hungarian horsemen have long excelled. Both types of Nonius combine active paces with a calm, willing temperament.

❚ BELOW
The head, though lacking refinement, reflects the breed's kind, tractable nature.

❚ BELOW
Thoroughbred, Norman and Norfolk Roadster blood all played a part in the development of the Nonius. Today's sturdily built individuals make good all-round riding and driving horses.

INTERESTING FACTS

There are two distinct types of harness used for driving purposes. These Nonius horses are wearing breast harness. For pulling heavy loads horses wear collars to enable them to use the full strength of their shoulders.

Hungarian Half-bred

The Hungarians began producing leisure and sports horses during the 1960s, continuing their tradition of breeding fine horses. They imported Hanoverians and Holsteins to cross with the Furioso and the Gidran in order to develop an animal suited to modern requirements. The Gidran, which to all intents and purposes is the Hungarian Anglo-Arab, can be traced back to an Arabian stallion known as Gidran Senior, imported into Hungary in 1816. Gidran's son, Gidran II, bred from a Spanish mare, became the foundation sire of the type which bears his name.

Initially a variety of mares were used, but later Thoroughbred blood was introduced and, subsequently, more Arab blood. This breeding policy

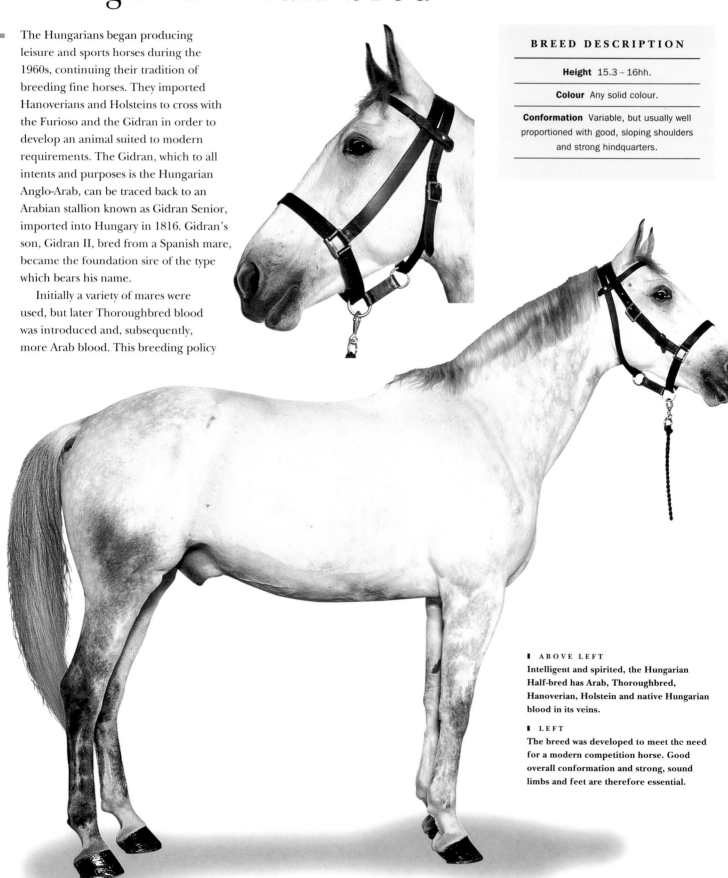

BREED DESCRIPTION

Height 15.3 – 16hh.

Colour Any solid colour.

Conformation Variable, but usually well proportioned with good, sloping shoulders and strong hindquarters.

▌ ABOVE LEFT
Intelligent and spirited, the Hungarian Half-bred has Arab, Thoroughbred, Hanoverian, Holstein and native Hungarian blood in its veins.

▌ LEFT
The breed was developed to meet the need for a modern competition horse. Good overall conformation and strong, sound limbs and feet are therefore essential.

INTERESTING FACTS

The Hungarian Half-bred has a good temperament which lends itself to training for a wide variety of activities – as this daring trick riding display proves.

■ LEFT
Speed, stamina and a ground-covering stride make the half-bred a suitable partner for the tough sport of three-day eventing.

■ BELOW
Hungarian Half-breds have achieved their greatest competition successes in the gruelling sport of four-in-hand driving. They have been exported to many countries for this purpose.

resulted in a quality horse with a good, ground-covering gallop. The breed was developed at Hungary's chief studs – the old-established one at Mezöhegyes; the Kisber, named after the Hungarian-bred horse who won the British Derby in 1876, and the Kecskemet, which is famous for its cross-bred driving horses, based on Lipizzaner and trotter blood.

Hungarian Half-breds have achieved outstanding success in the sport of international four-in-hand driving, where they have competed not just in the hands of the traditionally dashing and skilful Hungarian drivers but also for a number of other European nations, notably Switzerland and Britain.

Shagya

The Shagya is a strain of Arabian horse bred in Hungary and descended from a stallion of the same name. Shagya was a Syrian-bred horse, foaled in 1830 and imported to the Hungarian stud at Babolna some six years later. Shagya was used to cover quality mares which, although they were of mixed blood (including Hungarian, Thoroughbred and Spanish, as well as Arabian) were distinctly "eastern" in overall appearance. By employing the practice of inbreeding, the Babolna Stud produced the distinctive type of Arab horse seen today. The Shagya is rather taller and has a noticeably bigger frame than other Arabs (Shagya himself

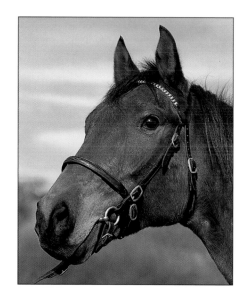

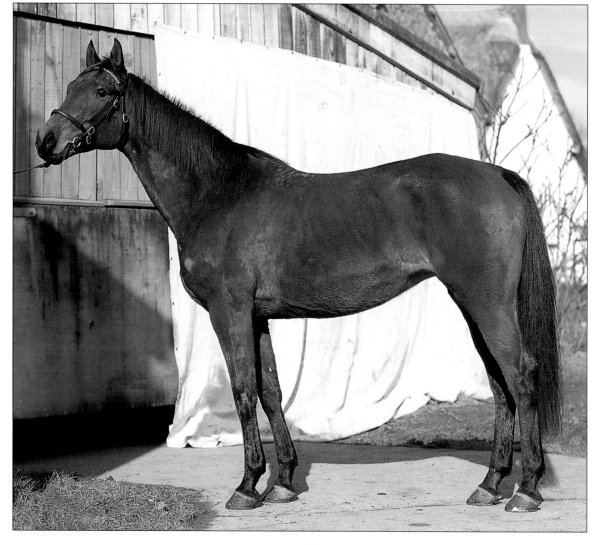

■ ABOVE LEFT
The wide-set eyes and tapered muzzle, with its large nostrils, are typical of the Shagya.

■ LEFT
The Shagya tends to have a rather more substantial frame than the pure-bred Arab, though its overall outline is very similar.

this barn is very ornate

was a little taller than normal for an Arab, standing over 15.2hh). But the overall appearance, with its beautiful, dished face, large eyes, short back and high-set tail, are all characteristic of the pure-bred Arab. Combining toughness with elegance, the Shagya was bred as a riding horse and found favour as a cavalry mount in the days before mechanization. Nowadays it is bred for leisure riding and is exported to a number of countries.

▮ ABOVE
Mares and foals at the Babolna Stud in Hungary, home of the Shagya Arab. Babolna was founded by Royal decree more than 200 years ago.

▮ BELOW
Grey is the breed's predominant colour, although all other Arab colours also occur. Shagya Arabs often stand a little taller than their pure-bred relatives.

Icelandic

The little Icelandic horse is probably the purest horse breed in the world. Its ancestors were taken to Iceland by ninth-century settlers, travelling from western Norway and the north of Britain. They were small, sturdy horses who adapted well to the rigorous Icelandic climate. Later some imports were made of eastern horses, but these had such a detrimental effect upon the original stock that in AD 930 the Althing (parliament) passed a law forbidding the import of further horses. Although this law seems to have been flouted occasionally, for the last 800 years there have been no infusions of outside blood. As a result the Icelandic

horse has changed little since the age of the Vikings.

It is an outstandingly tough, weather-resistant little horse (although it stands no more than 13.2hh it is always referred to by the Icelanders as a horse, not a pony). A strong swimmer – there were no bridges over Iceland's numerous turbulent rivers until the beginning of this century – it is also remarkably sure-footed. It can be seen carrying a full-grown man at speed, with ease and safety, over mountainous terrain during the traditional autumn sheep round-ups.

Some Icelandic horses are noted for their keen sense of direction and

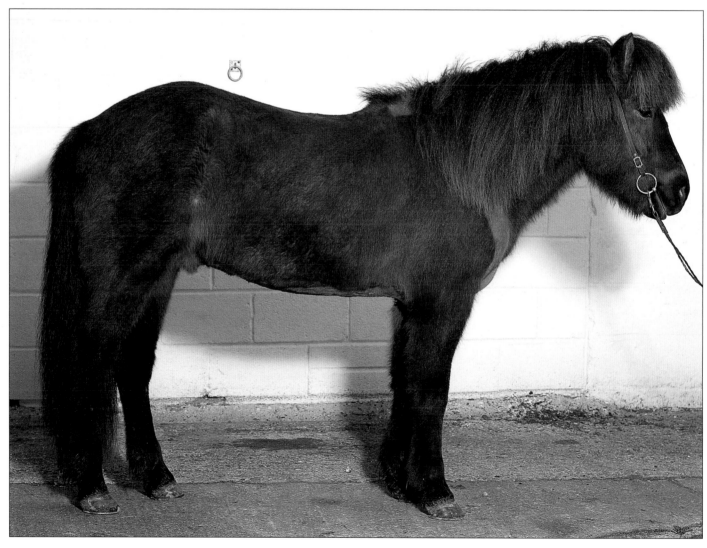

▮ LEFT
Icelandic Horses, which have changed little since Viking times, come in a wide range of attractive coat colours, including dun, palomino, piebald and skewbald.

BREED DESCRIPTION

Height 12.3 – 13.2hh.

Colour Any.

Conformation Fairly heavy head; short, well-carried neck; compact body with short back and deep girth; sloping, wedge-shaped, very strong, muscular hindquarters; strong limbs with short cannons and strong hocks; strong, well-shaped feet.

extraordinary homing instinct. After the annual round-up, while sheep are penned and sorted into each farmer's flock, horses are often turned loose and will set off alone down the valleys to their homes. There are also many recorded instances of horses that have been sold to another part of the country travelling for weeks to return to their original homes.

While some local selection of breeding stock probably took place from time to time, it was not until 1879 that Iceland undertook a practical selective breeding programme. It was begun in Skagafjördur, the country's most famous horse-breeding area. Conformation is naturally taken into account, but it is the quality of the horse's gaits which is of prime importance. These are: the fetgangur (walk), the brökk (trot – used when crossing rough country), the stökk (gallop), the skeid (lateral pace – used to cover short distances at high

speed) and the tölt (a running walk used to cover broken ground).The tölt is a gait of four equal beats – the sequence being near hind, near fore, off hind, off fore – with which the horse achieves great speed.

▮ BELOW
Notwithstanding its diminutive size, the breed is immensely strong and fast. It is a popular all-round riding horse in many countries outside its native Iceland.

INTERESTING FACTS

In days gone by horse fights were a popular form of entertainment in Iceland. Playing on the natural instinct of stallions to fight each other for possession of a mare, Icelanders would set two specially trained stallions against one another, using goads to urge them on. This pastime was so dangerous that it was a common occurrence for handlers to be injured or even killed.

Irish Draught

Irish horses are renowned for being the best hunters in the world and none more so than those produced by crossing the Thoroughbred with the versatile Irish Draught. Although there are no early formal records or stud books, Ireland's light draught horse is known to trace back many centuries, to the time when Norman horses were introduced to Ireland and crossed with the native animals, which at

▌ LEFT
A typically handsome, intelligent Irish Draught head. The breed is renowned for its innate good sense, coupled with boldness and athleticism.

that time were small of stature. Later infusions of Andalusian – and, probably, eastern – blood helped improve the overall quality (and height) of the Irish horses. The result was

very much an all-round horse, totally suited to the Irish country way of life: capable of working on the small Irish farms but active enough to be harnessed to a trap or to carry a rider safely across country. The modern Irish Draught is generally accepted to have evolved from the crossing of imported Thoroughbred stallions with the best of these country-bred mares. The numbers of these splendid horses declined in Ireland following the famine of 1847 and some heavy horses were introduced from Britain, but this tended to lead to a coarsening of the Irish Draught. To save the best of the remaining stock, in the early years of this century a scheme of subsidies was introduced by the government, for approved stallions of Irish Draught and hunter type. As a result the active, clean-legged general-purpose

▌ RIGHT
Substance and plenty of bone are the hallmarks of the modern Irish Draught. The conformation should incorporate all the features of the correctly built riding horse.

BREED DESCRIPTION

Height Stallions 16hh and over. Mares 15.2hh and over.

Colour All solid colours.

Conformation Small, intelligent head; sloping shoulders; strong body with deep chest and oval rib cage; powerful hindquarters; strong limbs with plenty of flat bone and no feather.

■ **LEFT**
As a safe conveyance across the most testing of hunting countries, there is nothing to beat the Irish Draught and the Irish Draught/ Thoroughbred cross.

■ **BELOW LEFT**
The international show jumper Mill Pearl: a good example of the Irish Draught cross with the ability to perform at the highest level.

■ **BELOW**
The breed possesses good, natural balance and the action is straight and true.

Irish Draught horse survived and in 1917 the Department of Agriculture introduced "a scheme to establish a Book for Horses of the Irish Draught type", in which 375 mares and 44 stallions were entered as being suitable and sound. The Irish Draught Horse Society was formed in 1976.

The excellence of Irish-bred horses owes much to the limestone pastures on which they are raised. The mineral-rich land contributes to the growth of strong bone and the production of good, up-standing animals. Today's Irish Draught has plenty of substance but is also an attractive looking, well-balanced, quality horse, with straight, athletic action. It is noted for its intelligence and kind temperament. It has an inherent ability to cross the most testing of hunting country with total assurance and because of its jumping prowess is a successful producer of top-level show jumpers.

INTERESTING FACTS

Since World War II many of the world's leading show-jumping horses have been Irish bred, with a fair percentage being by registered Irish Draught stallions. One of the most famous names in show-jumping breeding is King of Diamonds, an Irish Draught who sired many famous horses, including Special Envoy – who has jumped with great success for Brazil, ridden first by Nelson Pessoa then by his son Rodrigo – and Mill Pearl, ridden by the United States Olympic champion Joe Fargis.

Maremmano

Maremmano horses are bred in Tuscany and are the traditional mounts of the *butteri*, or cattlemen. Maremma, a coastal tract on the Tyrrhenian Sea extending from Piombino to Orbetello, is a former marshland which was drained in ancient times but later reverted to being an unhealthy wasteland. Drainage was reintroduced earlier this century and the area is now used as pastureland.

The origins of the Maremmano horses are obscure but it is likely that they are descended from the Neapolitan horses (founded on Arab, Barb and Spanish

■ RIGHT
The Maremmano is a strong horse possessed of a quiet temperament, and although not particularly speedy it makes a useful all-round riding horse.

blood) made famous in the sixteenth century by Federico Grisone. Grisone was the founder of the Neapolitan riding academy and regarded as the first of the great classical riding masters after the

Greek, Xenophon (c. 430–350 BC). A good deal of outcrossing took place later – some involving imported English horses, including the Norfolk Roadster – so that the horses which became known as the

■ LEFT
Maremmano horses vary a good deal in type and conformation. This horse is much more refined than many examples of the breed, with an especially elegant head.

▌ BELOW
A Maremmano wearing the traditional tack of the
buttero, or Italian cowboy. Its toughness and
reliability make the breed an ideal mount for
working with cattle.

BREED DESCRIPTION

Height Variable, usually around 15.3hh.

Colour Any solid colour.

Conformation Variable. Overall appearance
somewhat coarse, with rather upright
shoulders, flat withers and low-set tail,
though conformational improvements are
being made through the introduction of
Thoroughbred blood.

Maremmano were something of a mixture
and of no fixed type. By no means the
most beautiful looking of horses, nor the
speediest, they are nevertheless good,
honest workers, combining strength and
toughness with a calm temperament.
Amenable by nature and economical to
feed, they have proved useful as army and
police horses, as well as in agriculture –
they are strong enough to perform light
draught work – and cattle herding.

INTERESTING FACTS

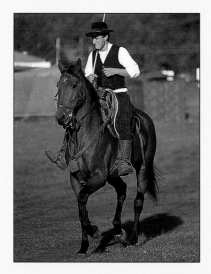

During the seventeenth century Italy became
one of the world leaders for horse breeding.
Most famous of all was the Neapolitan, of
which the Maremmano is possibly a descendant.

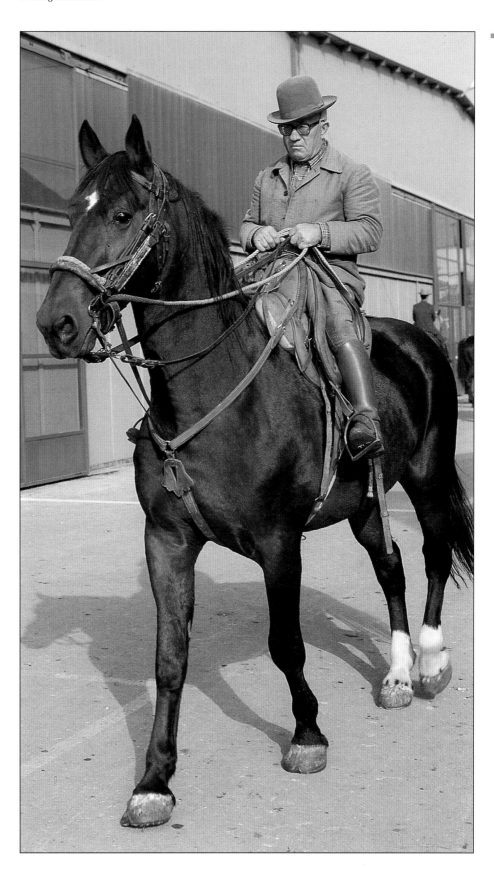

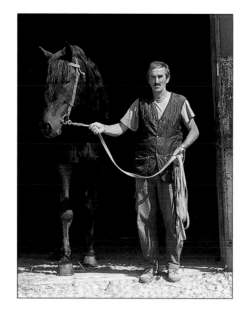

Murgese

Originating from the Orfano plain and the hill districts near Gravina, the original Murgese horse can be traced back at least 500 years. During the late fifteenth and early sixteenth centuries the governor of the port of Monopoli, which for some years belonged to the Venetian Republic, kept a stock of Murgese stallions and several hundred brood mares in order to provide remounts for the cavalry. However, somewhere down the years the breed died out and the modern version dates only from the 1920s.

The Murgese is basically a light draught horse, though inferior in quality to the Irish Draught and showing no great uniformity of type. It can be ridden, but a better stamp of riding horse is produced by putting a Murgese mare to a Thoroughbred or warmblood stallion, the latter giving the progeny more quality, and paces better suited to a saddle horse.

INTERESTING FACTS

The breeding of warmblood horses for present-day leisure and sport use is less advanced in Italy than in some other European countries, but an Italian Saddle Horse is gradually being evolved by crossing the best stock from the country's existing saddle breeds and types and crossing them with imported warmbloods and Thoroughbreds. Horses being merged in this way include the Salerno, which traces back to Neapolitan stock, and which also has Andalusian, Arab and Thoroughbred blood in its veins, and the Sardinian and Sicilian Anglo-Arabs.

BREED DESCRIPTION

Height 15 – 16hh.

Colour Usually chestnut, though other solid colours occur.

Conformation Variable. Overall appearance suggests a light draught horse. The head tends to be plain, though with an honest expression, and the hindquarters rather poor, with a low-set tail.

▮ **ABOVE**
Although basically best suited to light draught work, the Murgese can make a useful riding horse. This example of the breed has been fully trained as a police horse.

▮ **TOP LEFT**
Although the predominant coat colouring is chestnut, some dark colours do occur.

▮ **LEFT**
The Murgese is Italy's breed of light draught horse. However, it lacks definitive type and the overall quality of the light draught horse of Ireland.

Italian Heavy Draught

Italy's premier heavy horse, the Italian Heavy Draught – also known as the Agricultural Heavy Horse – bears a distinct resemblance to the handsome Breton, which has had an important influence upon its development. The Italian Heavy Draught originated at Ferrara in the north of the country during the second half of the nineteenth century, when Neapolitan blood was crossed with Arab and Hackney

BREED DESCRIPTION

Height Stallions 15 – 16hh.
Mares 14 – 15hh.

Colour Predominantly chestnut with flaxen mane and tail. Occasionally dark bay.

Conformation Square head with broad forehead, large eyes and nostrils and small, mobile ears; muscular, slightly arched neck; well-sloped shoulders; deep chest, short, strong back with broad, slightly sloping croup; short strong limbs with muscular forearms and large joints, short pasterns and large, well-shaped feet.

■ BOTTOM LEFT
The head is small with a straight profile. The eyes are large and bright, the ears small and mobile.

■ BELOW
Chestnut coat colouring with a flaxen mane and tail is typical of this attractive breed. It has inherited the active paces of the Breton, which had an important influence on its development.

to produce an active, lightweight workhorse. In due course the need arose both for a heavier agricultural animal and a heavy artillery horse, and breeders accordingly began introducing new blood, notably Boulonnais. Then, in the 1920s, pure-bred Breton stallions were used to establish the stamp of horse now known as the Italian Heavy Draught.

An attractive looking horse, stocky and muscular in build, the Italian Heavy Draught is noted for its conformation and active paces. It is capable of maintaining a good speed even when pulling heavy loads. The limbs are short and very strong with well-developed muscles and large joints. Although the need for draught horses has decreased in Italy, as elsewhere, the Italian Heavy Draught can still be seen at work on some of the smaller farms, and is also used for meat production.

INTERESTING FACTS

A stud book for Italian Draught Horses was opened in 1961. Horses accepted for registration are branded on the nearside of the hindquarters with the breed mark, a five-runged ladder within a shield.

Friesian

The Friesian is one of Europe's oldest horses and down the centuries it has had an influence on a number of other breeds, notably the Oldenburg in Germany and Britain's Fell and Dales ponies. The breed's homeland is Friesland, in the

 LEFT
The Friesian's friendly disposition is evident in its kind but alert expression. The rather long head is set on a well-arched neck.

north of the Netherlands. The remains of an ancient coldblood type of heavy horse have been unearthed there, from which the modern Friesian is believed to be descended. Eastern blood, introduced into the Netherlands during the time of

BREED DESCRIPTION

Height 15 – 16hh.

Colour Always black.

Conformation Rather long head, with short ears and alert expression; elegant, arched neck with long, flowing mane; powerful shoulders; strong, compact body with strong, sloping hindquarters and rather low-set, very full, tail; short, strong limbs with good bone and a fair amount of feather.

 RIGHT
Excellent overall conformation is the hallmark of the breed. The body is compact, the limbs strong and the feet hard and sound.

■ LEFT
An attractive turnout much appreciated throughout its native land: a Friesian driven to a traditional high-wheeled gig.

■ BELOW
Appreciation of Friesians is not restricted to Holland. This handsome team was pictured in a busy London street.

The Friesians' noble bearing makes them ideal for ceremonial occasions. These horses were part of a six-strong team pulling the Dutch Royal Carriage at the opening ceremony of the 1994 World Equestrian Games in The Hague.

the Crusades, had an influence on the development of the Friesian, as did the Andalusian during the Eighty Years' War, when the Netherlands were occupied by the Spanish. The Friesian horse which thus developed was an active all-rounder, suitable for work on the land but, because of its ability to trot at speed, also useful as a harness horse and for riding.

During the nineteenth century, when trotting became extremely popular, breeders sought to improve the Friesian's already active, high-stepping trot, by outcrossing to trotters. This led to the Friesian becoming lighter in build and less useful as a farm horse. By the beginning of World War I its numbers were seriously depleted and the decline continued between the wars. However, lack of fuel during World War II led to a revival in the breed's fortunes as farmers once again turned to it for draught work.

During the second half of this century there has been a resurgence of interest in the breed and it is now very popular as a carriage horse. A well-balanced horse with proud bearing, the Friesian looks exceptionally attractive when pulling a traditional high-wheeled Friesian gig. The breed is noted for its kind temperament.

Po not ride horses in places like this. Many accidents happen.

Gelderland

A number of different breeds went into the making of the Gelderland, which comes from the region of the same name in the central Netherlands and was developed during the nineteenth century. Native mares were crossed with, among others, English, French, German, Hungarian and Polish stallions to produce a good stamp of dual-purpose horse, one that was big and strong enough to do farm work or pull a carriage but not so heavy that it could not be used for riding. Hackney blood was also used in a

Strong and active, the Gelderland makes an excellent carriage horse and has also played a part in the development of Holland's remarkably successful competition horse, the Dutch Warmblood.

INTERESTING FACTS

The Gelderland is one of two types of all-purpose horse developed in the Netherlands, the other being its northern neighbour, the Gröningen. The Gröningen is somewhat heavier than the Gelderland. It has Friesian and Oldenburg blood in its ancestry, as well as some Suffolk Punch. Like the Gelderland, it has played an important part in the development of the Dutch Warmblood.

breeding programme that was noted for its well-founded principles of selection, only horses that had proved themselves to be good, sound workers being used at stud. As mechanization spread, and horses were needed less for use on the land, breeders introduced Thoroughbred blood to lighten the Gelderland.

A typical carriage type of horse, the modern Gelderland, with its excellent shoulders and good, free action, has been used successfully in the sport of four-in-hand driving and has also provided one of the main bases for the production of the Netherlands' sports horse, the Dutch Warmblood.

■ RIGHT
Good shoulders are a characteristic of Gelderland conformation, ensuring free movement at all paces.

BREED DESCRIPTION

Height About 16hh.

Colour Predominantly chestnut, sometimes bay or grey.

Conformation Rather plain, sensible looking head, with a tendency to a convex profile; strong neck; good shoulders, with fairly low withers; fairly long but strong body with good depth through the girth; powerful hindquarters with high-set tail; short, strong limbs with good, sound feet.

Dutch Warmblood

The production of the Netherlands' highly successful leisure and competition horse began with the selection of the best Gelderland and Gröningen mares, who were then mated with Thoroughbred stallions. The latter, also carefully selected, were imported from all over the world, including Britain, Ireland, France and the United States. Many of these came from the best racing lines, a fact which was to prove highly beneficial: as time went on Dutch breeders found that the stallions

BREED DESCRIPTION

Height 16 – 17hh.

Colour Any solid colour, with bay and brown the most usual.

Conformation Quality head, with alert, intelligent expression; good, sloping shoulders with pronounced withers; strong back and hindquarters; good, sound limbs, with plenty of bone and short cannons; good, sound feet.

▌ LEFT
Milton is a grandson of the Trakehner Marco Polo, one of the most influential Dutch Warmblood stallions.

INTERESTING FACTS

One of the most important stallions in the breeding of Dutch Warmbloods was the Trakehner Marco Polo (1965–1976). By the Thoroughbred Poet, he was only small but he produced some top-class show jumpers. They included Marius, who was ridden with great international success by Britain's Caroline Bradley. In Britain Marius combined his competitive career with stud duties and had the distinction of siring Milton, the world's most successful show jumper.

Dutch breeders use a highly efficient, performance-based selection system to produce their horses and, despite its relative newness, the Dutch Warmblood has already demonstrated the correctness of their approach by achieving success at top international level in dressage, show jumping and carriage driving. Dutch

Warmbloods have been used in the establishment of other warmblood strains, too, notably in Britain, the United States, Australia and New Zealand.

who produced the best warmbloods had themselves enjoyed successful racing careers. In addition to Thoroughbreds, some Trakehner stallions were used in the early years, and a number of Holstein mares were imported and put to Gelderland or Gröningen stallions. Later on warmbloods of the type which the Dutch breeders were seeking to develop, such as the Holstein and Selle Français, were introduced into the breeding programme, and a dash of Hanoverian and Westphalian blood was added. At the same time there was a gradual decrease in the amount of Gelderland and Gröningen blood used. The result is a riding horse of harmonious proportions, with straight, true action, an easy, ground-covering stride at all paces and a good temperament.

▌ LEFT
The Dutch Warmblood is a quality horse possessed of a good temperament. The correct proportions of its conformation result in excellent action, thus ensuring its suitability for modern competitive sports.

Lusitano

As its appearance suggests, the Portuguese Lusitano is a close relative of the Andalusian in neighbouring Spain. Indeed, until quite recent times the horses bred on the Iberian peninsula were regarded as being one and the same. It was not until the early years of the twentieth century that the two countries decided to establish independent stud books.

Since opening their own stud book the Portuguese have made great strides in monitoring and improving their breeding programme. They have been diligent in preserving the Lusitano's greatly admired qualities of strength and courage. These attributes led to the breed being very highly esteemed as a warhorse (the best Iberian horses have always been bred along the long frontier between

BREED DESCRIPTION

Height Generally 15.1 – 15.3hh. Some horses reach over 16hh.

Colour Often grey or bay, but any true colour is found, including dun and chestnut.

Conformation Long, noble head, typically with a convex profile, finely curved nose and large, generous eyes; powerful, arched neck, deep at the base and set at a slightly wide angle to the shoulders, giving the impression of being fairly upright; powerful shoulders; short-coupled body with deep rib cage, broad, powerful loins, gently sloping croup and rather low-set tail; fine, clean legs with excellent dense bone; abundant silky mane and tail.

Portugal and Spain where endless battles were fought).

These same qualities also make the Lusitano an ideal mount for the demanding sport of mounted bullfighting. In Portugal, where it is considered a disgrace for a horse to be injured during a bullfight, the horses are extremely well

trained, using their inherent powers of acceleration and manoeuvrability to evade the bull.

As they have proved down the centuries, Lusitano horses are most amenable to training. Intelligent, gentle and affectionate, they work hard and enthusiastically. Possessed of good natural

▌ABOVE LEFT
This noble head and powerful, arched neck are characteristic of the Lusitano. The breed is also noted for its silky mane and tail.

▌LEFT
The overall outline of the Lusitano is virtually the same as that of its close relative, the Andalusian.

INTERESTING FACTS

The Lusitano horse gives an exceptionally smooth, comfortable ride. Agile and intelligent, it makes the ideal mount for the mounted bullfighter.

balance and with agile, elevated paces, they give a smooth comfortable ride. With their proud bearing and tremendous joie de vivre they have, not surprisingly, always excelled at high school work. However, it is not only in the manège that the breed excels. More and more Lusitanos are proving themselves well suited to modern sports such as show jumping and carriage driving. People who work with them testify to the great understanding which quickly develops between horse and human.

ALTER REAL

The Alter Real is not a distinct breed but an offshoot of the Lusitano. It takes its name from the town of Alter do Chão, in the Portuguese province of Alentejo, the world "real" meaning royal in Portuguese. The royal stud founded at Alter supplied the royal manège in Lisbon with high-school and carriage horses. The stud flourished for many years, producing a fine line of horses which were valued not

only in Portugal but all over the Peninsula. However, the stud's progress suffered serious interruption on a number of occasions, notably during the Peninsular War, and the Alter Real horses went into decline. Attempts to resurrect the strain towards the end of the nineteenth century by importing English, Norman and German blood were not successful, nor was a subsequent attempt, using Arab horses. Through the introduction of Andalusian blood at the end of the century, the Alter Real Lusitanos were finally re-established but after the fall of the monarchy in the early twentieth century, many horses were sold or destroyed. The Alter Real line would have died out but for the efforts of the d'Andrade family, who during the early 1940s saved two stallions and a handful of mares and instigated a breeding programme. Today the Alter Stud is state run and again produces horses for high school work. The Alter Real is essentially a Lusitano, although it is always bay, brown or black in colour.

Bashkir

The small Bashkir horse comes from the southern foothills of the Ural mountains, taking its name from the region of Bashkirsky where it is kept in herds. It goes equally well in harness and under saddle and for centuries has been used as a pack and general work horse as well as a supplier of meat and milk. Stockily built,

BREED DESCRIPTION

Height 13.3 – 14hh.

Colour Predominantly bay, chestnut and brown.

Conformation Massive head; short, fleshy neck; low withers; wide, deep body with broad, straight back; comparatively short legs with substantial bone; good, hard feet.

with a thick coat, mane and tail, it can survive in the open in temperatures as low as -22° to -40° Fahrenheit (-30° to -40° C). It is able to withstand ferocious blizzard conditions and will dig through snow a metre deep to find food. Furthermore, its tremendously hard feet enable it to work without being shod. The Bashkir is undoubtedly one of the hardiest breeds of

horse or pony in the world.

A type of Bashkir also exists in the north-west of the United States, prompting the theory that these horses' ancestors travelled over the former land-bridge between Asia and North America (now the Bering Strait). The horse, however, is generally believed to have become extinct on the North American continent as long ago as the Ice Age and was not reintroduced until Spanish explorers of the modern era "discovered" the land. It is therefore much more likely that the Bashkir was introduced from Russia in fairly recent times.

▌ **ABOVE LEFT**
The Bashkir's head is heavily built and set on a short, fleshy neck. The chest is broad.

▌ **LEFT**
With its stocky build, short strong limbs and exceptionally hard feet, the Bashkir is well equipped for life in a harsh environment – though, as this picture shows, it also thrives in less rigorous surroundings.

Don

Don horses were made famous by the Don Cossacks, who between 1812 and 1814 helped drive Napoleon's invading troops from Russia. The Cossacks' horses were descended from those of the nomadic steppe people and were of mixed blood. Early influences would have included the Nagai from Mongolia, the Karabakh (a type of light riding horse), the Turkmen and the Persian Arab. During the nineteenth century infusions of Orlov and Thoroughbred blood were made and outcrosses were also made to the part-bred Arab horses produced at the Strelets Stud in the Ukraine. All these crosses, used to upgrade the old Cossack strain, ceased at the beginning of this century, since when no more outside blood has been used in the breeding of Don horses.

Like most Russian breeds, the Don was traditionally reared in herds on the vast expanses of the steppes, and accordingly developed into a tough individual, capable of thriving with minimal help from humans. It was ideally suited to its original role as an army remount while nowadays it is used for general riding purposes.

Various inherent conformational defects tend to limit the quality of its paces but its strong constitution makes it a suitable mount for endurance riding.

■ TOP
Don horses are predominantly chestnut. Calm and willing workers, they go equally well in harness and under saddle and have great endurance.

■ ABOVE
The Don tends to lack good riding horse conformation: straight shoulders and rather upright pasterns are common faults.

BREED DESCRIPTION

Height 15.3 – 16.2hh.

Colour Predominantly chestnut and brown, often with a golden sheen.

Conformation Medium-sized head with wide forehead; average length neck; strong body with broad, straight back and loins and rounded croup; rather sloping hindquarters; straight limbs with well-muscled forearms and second thighs, but a tendency to calf knees (an inward curve below the knee), sickle hocks and upright pasterns; short, thin mane and tail.

Budenny

A breed of relatively recent origin, the Budenny was created by crossing Don and Chernomor mares with Thoroughbred stallions (the Chernomor was the horse used by Cossacks who settled in the Kuban during the eighteenth century and was similar to the Don, though somewhat smaller and lighter in build). The chief purpose was to produce a good army remount, possessed of great endurance. Breeding was centred in the Rostov region, using a process of careful selection. The best mares were bred to the

Russian horses are often hot branded as an aid to identification. The chestnut horse on the facing page has also been freeze-branded on the saddle patch. This is a valuable form of individual identity marking which helps to deter horse thieves because the owner can easily be traced.

▌ ABOVE RIGHT
The Thoroughbred influence on the present-day Budenny is particularly noticeable in the refinement of head, with its lean good looks, bright, intelligent eyes and alert ears.

▌ RIGHT
The overall conformation, while showing good depth through the girth and a reasonably well-sloped shoulder, lacks the harmonious proportions of the Thoroughbred, notably in the hind limbs, which are inclined to be a bit weak.

best Anglo-Don stallions. The brood mares were both well fed and, unusually in Russian horse breeding at the time, stabled during the worst of the winter weather, thus ensuring that they produced better, healthier foals than they might otherwise have done if forced to burn up their resources merely on keeping themselves warm. The young stock were tested on the racecourse between two and four years of age.

The robust constitution of the Don horse and the excellent action of the Thoroughbred proved to be a good combination and as a result the Rostov military stud farm was soon turning out an

BREED DESCRIPTION

Height 16hh.

Colour Predominantly chestnut, some bay and brown. The coats of some Budenny horses have a golden sheen (a throwback to the Chernomor and Don horses).

Conformation Well-proportioned head with straight or slightly concave profile; long, straight neck; reasonably well-sloped shoulders with high withers; comparatively heavy body with short, straight back and long croup; fine, straight limbs, though with a tendency to small joints and rather weak hindlegs; usually well-shaped feet.

upstanding horse, with a tractable nature, which proved suitable for both riding and light draught work. Named the Budenny, it was officially recognized as a breed in 1949.

As the need for army remounts ceased and interest turned to pleasure riding and sport, more Thoroughbred was added to improve the Budenny. Although the Thoroughbred influence is quite evident in the overall light build, the Budenny has a noticeably heavier body while the legs tend to be a bit light on bone. Today the breed is used as a general purpose riding horse, especially in the sports of show jumping, dressage and steeplechasing.

∎ RIGHT
The predominant Budenny coat colouring is chestnut. Some horses have a striking golden sheen.

Kabardin

Sure-footedness and a well-developed sense of self-preservation are the hallmarks of the Kabardin and little wonder, for its home is the northern Caucasus, where it has for centuries been accustomed to carrying men over the toughest mountain terrain. It traces back

■ ABOVE
The Kabardin's head is long and Roman noses are not uncommon. The ears are very mobile and the horse has a kind, calm expression.

BREED DESCRIPTION

Height 15 – 15.2hh.

Colour Predominantly bay, dark bay and black, usually without distinguishing markings.

Conformation Long head, often with Roman-nosed profile, with sharp, mobile ears; well-muscled, medium-long neck; fairly straight shoulders and low withers; strong body, with short, straight back and short, often concave loins; strong limbs, with generally good joints, good bone and short, strong cannons, although the hindlegs tend to be sickle-shaped; good, strong feet; usually long, full mane and tail.

INTERESTING FACTS

The Kabardin's prowess at carrying a rider safely over mountainous terrain is legendary. It will pick its way unerringly over narrow, rocky mountain tracks with all the assurance of a mountain goat and has an uncanny ability to find its way in the mist or dark. Its typical mountain-horse conformation may not be conducive to speed, but its paces are nevertheless cadenced, light and smooth.

to the sixteenth century and is derived from the horses of the steppe tribes who were crossed with Turkmen, Persian and Karabakh horses. Originally the Kabardin was itself fairly small. Raised in herds, which were (and still are) grazed on the

■ RIGHT
Having evolved in the mountains, Kabardin horses are very athletic and well balanced. They make good jumpers.

■ RIGHT
Despite rather straight shoulders, Kabardins make good all-round riding horses. They are agile and sure-footed.

high pastures during the summer and in the foothills during the winter, it developed into a typical mountain breed: tough, sturdy and possessing great endurance.

The numbers of Kabardin horses were seriously depleted as a result of the Revolution and it was during the 1920s, when efforts were made to re-establish the breed, that a bigger stamp of horse began to be produced, one suitable as an army remount and for agricultural work. The Malokarachaev and Malkin Studs became the producers of the best modern Kabardin horses, which are used to improve stock in neighbouring areas as well as for general riding and driving purposes.

Tersk

Like the Kabardin, the Tersk comes from the northern Caucasus, though it is a breed of more recent origin, having been developed from 1921 onwards at the Tersk and Stavropol Studs.

The Tersk is based on Strelets horses, the part-bred Arabs which were formerly bred at the Strelets Stud in the Ukraine. The Strelets was produced by crossing

BREED DESCRIPTION

Height Stallions 15hh. Mares 14.3hh.

Colour Predominantly light grey or "white" with a silvery sheen.

Conformation Fine head with large, expressive eyes and medium-length, mobile ears; medium-length neck set high on well-sloped shoulders; strong body with deep chest, wide back and muscular loins; fine legs with well-defined tendons; fine mane and tail.

INTERESTING FACTS

Nowadays most of the world's Tersk horses are produced at the Stavropol Stud. Stavropol is in the northern Caucasus between the Black Sea and the Caspian Sea.

▌ **BELOW**
Tersk horses are invariably refined and elegant. Their predominantly light grey colouring adds to their attraction.

▌ **BOTTOM**
The breed shows unmistakable signs of its Arab ancestry though it is usually a little taller than the pure-bred Arab.

pure-bred Arabs with, among others, high quality Orlovs and Anglo-Arabs (some Thoroughbred blood was also used, though this was not a dominant factor).

The result was a horse with a distinctly Arabian look about it but one which was bigger built than the pure-breds.

By the 1920s there were very few Strelets in existence. The few that did remain, including two stallions, were taken to the Tersk Stud in an attempt to increase their numbers. The mares were put to pure-bred Arab stallions; and various cross-bred mares, including Strelets x Kabardin and Arab x Don, were covered by the Strelets stallions. After some thirty years the new type, known as the Tersk, became fixed. It has inherited the general appearance of the Arab, though it stands a little taller, and also its elegant paces. A handsome horse, usually grey in colour, it combines a kind temperament with tremendous energy, attributes which have made it a favourite in circuses and also as a sports horse.

Orlov Trotter

The Orlov shares with the Standardbred and the French Trotter the distinction of being one of the world's foremost breeds of trotting horse. Indeed, before the development of the Standardbred it was probably the most famous of all trotters. Although the Orlov is less well known now outside its native land than the other two members of the triumvirate, it nevertheless plays an important role both in Russian harness racing and in the upgrading of other Russian breeds.

The Orlov takes its name from Count Alexis Orlov (1737–1809), founder of the Orlov Stud near Moscow. The Count imported from Greece a grey Arab stallion called Smetanka. Despite Smetanka's short stud career, he was to prove highly influential in the development of this popular breed. Smetanka's grey son

■ LEFT
The head of the Orlov Trotter is inclined to be coarse and rather small.

Polkan, bred out of a Danish mare and foaled in 1784, produced Bars I, who became the foundation sire of the Orlov Trotter.

The breed was developed by Count Orlov and his stud manager V.I. Shishkin at the then newly founded Khrenov Stud in the province of Voronezh

BREED DESCRIPTION

Height Stallions 16hh. Mares 15.3hh.

Colour Predominantly grey. Bay and black are commonly found. Chestnut is rare.

Conformation Small, often somewhat coarse head; long, often swan-shaped, neck set high on the withers; long, straight back with muscular loins and broad, powerful croup; fine, squarely set legs with a minimum of 8 inches (20cm) of bone below the knee.

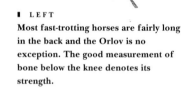

■ LEFT
Most fast-trotting horses are fairly long in the back and the Orlov is no exception. The good measurement of bone below the knee denotes its strength.

INTERESTING FACTS

Count Alexis Orlov, the breed's founder, was a soldier famous for his courage and audacity. In 1762 he played a part in the assassination of Peter III. The Count's older brother, Grigorei, who distinguished himself during the Seven Years' War, had attracted the attention of Peter's wife, soon to become Catherine II. However, having helped place her on the throne, Grigorei found himself ousted from the Empress's favour by his fellow conspirator, the handsome Prince Potemkin. Alexis is reputed to have knocked out Potemkin's eye – and turned to horse breeding as a diversion from affairs at court!

■ **RIGHT**
The Russian Trotter is part Orlov, part Standardbred. It is faster on the racetrack than the Orlov.

to which the stock from the Moscow stud was transferred in 1788. Bars I was used to breed from Arab, Dutch and Danish mares as well as half-breds imported from England. Inbreeding back to Bars I was practised extensively. During the early part of the nineteenth century the breed continued to improve thanks to the systematic training and racing of trotters in Russia.

Later, as the Standardbred began to demonstrate its supremacy on the racetrack, the Russians started importing horses from America to cross with the Orlov. The resultant half-breed, subsequently known as the Russian Trotter, proved faster than the Orlov. Imports of Standardbreds ceased at the outbreak of World War I but in recent times the traffic has resumed to maintain the speed of the Russian Trotter.

■ **BELOW**
As well as being raced in their native country, Orlovs are well suited to the modern sport of four-in-hand driving. They are exported for this purpose.

■ **BELOW**
This horse, hitched to a training vehicle, demonstrates the Orlov's tremendously powerful action.

Vladimir Heavy Draught

The Clydesdale played a significant part in the development of the Vladimir, a heavy draught horse created in the provinces of Vladimir and Ivanovo, to the north-east of Moscow. During the early years of this century stallions of various heavy breeds were imported from Britain and France to cross with the local mares of the region in order to produce a good-quality heavy work horse. Among the most influential of the foundation stallions were the Clydesdales Lord James, Border Brand, both imported in 1910, and Glen Albin (1923). Shire stallions were also used, though to a lesser extent, and some Cleveland Bay, Suffolk, Ardennais and

Percheron blood is also said to have been introduced. The experiment met with success, the result being a powerfully built heavy horse, well suited to all types of heavy agricultural and draught work. Named the Vladimir Heavy Draught, it was recognized as a breed in 1946.

Its docile nature makes it easy to handle, while its active paces – no doubt inherited from its Clydesdale forebears – mean that despite its massive build it can be used to pull the famous Russian troikas. Another bonus is its early maturity: the Vladimir is so well developed by the age of three that it can start work and also be used at stud, where the stallions are noted

▌ OPPOSITE ABOVE
The Vladimir Heavy Draught combines great strength with the most docile of natures – note this horse's kindly expression.

▌ OPPOSITE BELOW
Clydesdale blood was used with great success in the development of this breed, which is renowned for its powerful build and active paces.

BREED DESCRIPTION

Height Stallions 16.1hh. Mares 15.3hh.

Colour Predominantly bay, also black and chestnut with white markings on head and legs.

Conformation Large, long head with convex profile; long, muscular neck; pronounced withers; wide chest, rather long, broad back and long, broad, sloping croup; long limbs; some horses carry feather.

for their good fertility rate. Minus points include, in some horses, a rather long back, which is not conducive to strength, and a flat-sided rib cage (the reverse of "well sprung" or rounded ribs, which enable the lungs to work to maximum efficiency). The Vladimir is the largest of the Russian heavy breeds. Stallions have a girth of some 6 feet 9 inches (207cm) and weigh in the region of 1,688lb (758kg). Mares are only a little smaller, with a girth of 6 feet 5 inches (196cm) and a weight of 1,507lb (685kg).

INTERESTING FACTS

Other heavy horses in the former USSR include the Russian Heavy Draught, founded a century or so ago, and based largely on the Ardennais, and the Soviet Heavy Draught, which was founded by crossing Belgian Heavy Draught stallions with local harness-type mares. Both were registered as breeds in 1952. The Russian Heavy Draught is quick to mature and remarkably long lived. It was formerly known as the "Russian Ardennes".

LATVIAN

The Latvian is a powerfully built harness horse renowned for its weight-pulling ability. It is of recent origin, dating only from the early 1920s when local mares were crossed with German, English and French horses to produce an all-round worker possessed of strength, stamina and good, active paces. There are two distinct types of Latvian horse: a heavy harness type which is based largely on Oldenburg, Norfolk Roadster and Anglo-Norman outcrosses and a lighter version which has a preponderance of Hanoverian blood.

Latvian horses have good overall conformation and great freedom of movement. Stallions stand up to 16.2hh, mares up to 16hh. Black is the predominant colour of the heavier type, while most of the lighter weight horses are chestnut.

The Latvian harness horse was recognized as a breed in 1952 and although some outcrosses to Oldenburg and Hanoverian horses have been made since, these have been on a fairly limited scale. The breed is especially noted for its placid temperament which, together with its strength and energy, make it a popular working animal.

North Swedish

Forestry is the chief area of employment for the North Swedish horse, a small, compact, agile draught horse ideally suited to moving timber in confined spaces, over difficult terrain and often in inclement weather conditions.

The breed is descended from the ancient native work horse of Sweden which was influenced by the Døle horses from neighbouring Norway. At some time during the nineteenth century, outcrosses were made to horses of lighter build from outside Scandinavia but towards the end of the century there was a move to produce a heavier stamp of horse, more suited to pulling the heavier types of machinery which were then becoming available. Consequently stallions from larger breeds, such as the Clydesdale, were imported.

BREED DESCRIPTION

Height Stallions around 15.2hh. Mares around 15hh.

Colour Any solid colour.

Conformation Fairly large head with longish ears; short, crested neck; strong, sloping shoulders; rather long, but deep, strong back; rounded hindquarters with sloping croup; short, strong limbs with good bone; the mane and tail are usually very abundant.

The possibility of the old Swedish horse dying out altogether as a result of these crosses prompted interested parties to form an association to save it, the aim being to breed from the old-type stock still found in the remoter parts of the north of the country, using Døle stallions. Government support during the early years of the twentieth century aided this aim and during the 1920s performance testing was introduced as a means of selection, something which is still used today. Horses are tested for their draught aptitude as well as draught efficiency. The former test involves pulling a sled laden with logs, the judges awarding points according to the horse's performance and its condition after the work. For the efficiency test the horse is hitched to a wagon and its actual pulling power is measured by a dynamometer.

Lumbering is an area where heavy horses can prove more efficient and more cost effective than mechanized transport, and the North Swedish Horse continues to thrive in its traditional environment.

▌ LEFT
Small and compact, the North Swedish horse is particularly strong through the neck and shoulders. Its short limbs have plenty of bone.

INTERESTING FACTS

North Swedish horses make good all-round draught animals. They are, however, most often associated with agricultural work and, more especially, forestry. They begin work as three-year-olds and within a couple of years are sufficiently mature to be capable of working an eight-hour day. Stallions weigh anything from 1,440 to 1,655lb (650–750kg) and mares 1,200 to 1,545lb (550–700kg).

Swedish Warmblood

Sweden has been renowned for its fine riding and carriage horses for many centuries, so it is not surprising that the Swedish Warmblood should have had such an impact on present-day competitive sports, particularly top-level dressage.

The Skåne province of what is now southern Sweden (the area had previously been under Danish rule) was noted for its horse breeding as long ago as the twelfth century, when Archbishop Absalon raised remounts there for his cavalry. Then in the mid-seventeenth century, Charles X of Sweden founded the Royal Stud at Flyinge, to the north-east of Malmo, to supply horses for the royal stables and the

army. Down the years horses from a wide variety of breeds were used at the stud to produce a quality cavalry horse. They included Holsteins, Hanoverians, East Prussians, Frederiksborgs, Arabs, Thoroughbreds and Oldenburgs, with the East Prussian and Hanoverian blood being particularly influential.

Officers of the Swedish cavalry mounted on Swedish horses enjoyed tremendous success in all three equestrian disciplines (dressage, show jumping and three-day eventing) at Olympic level both before and after World War I. The Swiss army bought many Swedish horses after World War II, a number of whom found fame in the dressage world. When mechanization signalled the demise of the cavalry horse it was a natural progression for the Swedes to channel their horse-breeding efforts towards leisure and

■ RIGHT
Warmblood mares with their foals put on a fine show to an appreciative crowd during the 1990 World Equestrian Games in Stockholm.

■ BOTTOM LEFT
Thanks to infusions of outside blood, including Thoroughbred, the breed has become a good all-round sports horse.

■ BOTTOM RIGHT
Swedish Warmbloods have traditionally excelled at the demanding discipline of Grand Prix dressage.

BREED DESCRIPTION

Height 15 – 17hh.

Colour Any solid colour.

Conformation Variable, but usually a handsome head, with wide forehead and kind, intelligent eyes; long neck; shoulders sometimes tend to be rather straight, depending on the bloodline; well-proportioned body, hindquarters and limbs.

INTERESTING FACTS

Swedish-bred dressage horses which have found fame at the Olympic Games include Piaff, winner of the individual gold medal in Munich in 1972, when ridden by the West German, Liselott Linsenhoff. Piaff's sire was Gaspari, who competed for Sweden in the 1960 Games in Rome, where another Swedish horse, Wald, won the individual silver medal in the hands of the Swiss rider, Gustav Fischer. In Tokyo in 1964 Fischer's compatriot, Henri Chammartin, was the individual gold medallist on yet another Swedish horse, Woermann. Also Swedish bred was Gauguin de Lully, winner of the individual bronze medal at the Seoul Games in 1988, again competing for Switzerland.

competition. There was no doubting the Swedish Warmblood's prowess as a dressage horse and in recent times top jumping blood has been introduced from France, Germany and Holland. Carefully selected Thoroughbred stallions have also been used on warmblood mares.

To maintain the excellence of the breed, in terms of both conformation and temperament, Swedish Warmblood stallions are graded and must pass a performance test, veterinary examination and assessment of type, conformation and action. There is also a system of progeny testing, the results of which are available to mare owners seeking a suitable stallion.

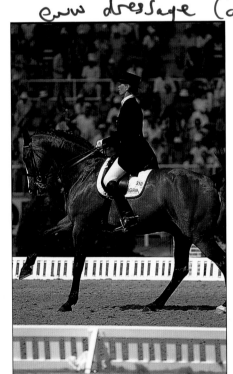

▌ LEFT
The Akhal-Teke's head is always very fine, with large expressive eyes and beautifully shaped ears.

Akhal-Teke

One of the most striking looking horses anywhere in the world, the Akhal-Teke, or Turkmen, has been bred for some 3,000 years in the desert oases of Turkmenistan, a region to the north of Iran and to the east of the Caspian Sea. Although the Turkmen people probably introduced a certain amount of Arabian and Persian blood at some stage, its isolated homeland has kept the Akhal-Teke freer from outside influences than many riding

▌ BELOW
The luminous sheen on the coat of this horse is typical of the breed, as is the lean overall appearance.

■ RIGHT
Akhal-Tekes make good all-round riding horses, their legendary stamina making them excellent mounts for competitive endurance riding.

■ BOTTOM RIGHT
Despite being raised for centuries in desert conditions, the breed adapts perfectly well to life in the much less rigorous climate of western Europe.

BREED DESCRIPTION

Height 15.1 – 15.2hh.

Colour Bay and chestnut, often with a remarkable golden sheen; also grey and black.

Conformation Very fine head with wide nostrils, large, expressive eyes and long, beautifully shaped ears; long, straight and often thin neck set high on the shoulders; sloping shoulder with high withers; long, often weak back, shallow rib cage and a tendency to poor loins, lacking in muscle; narrow hindquarters but with muscular croup and long, muscular thighs; strong, straight forelegs with long forearm, and long hindlegs which tend to be sickle shaped with cow hocks; small but hard feet; sparse mane and tail; thin skin.

horses. Raised to withstand the extreme conditions of the desert – fiercely hot days alternating with cold nights – the Akhal-Teke developed into a tough, lean horse, whose undoubted conformational defects are offset by its fast paces, stamina and tremendous hardiness. This hardiness owes much to the rigorous lifestyle imposed upon it over many centuries. The traditional Turkmen method of horse management did not included stabling. The animals were wrapped in felt, with only their heads uncovered, and kept on

INTERESTING FACTS

The Akhal-Teke used to be renowned for its devotion to its rider – which is not surprising if one tale told about the Turkmen training techniques is true. According to this story, a young horse would be kept alone in a pit or enclosure. Stones would be thrown at it by everyone but the owner. Only he would treat it kindly and offer it food. Thus the horse learnt to trust only one man and to fear all others. This could account for the breed's sometimes difficult temperament.

tethers. Their diet included meagre amounts of dry lucerne, barley and some mutton fat. Foals were weaned very young and the horses raced as yearlings. Nowadays Akhal-Tekes are kept along more modern lines, out at grass by day

and stabled by night. They are still raced, though not until they are two- or three-year-olds, as is the custom in the Thoroughbred racing world.

Spirited and athletic, they are used for general riding purposes, including show jumping and dressage, and at stud in the development of other riding horse breeds. Their phenomenal stamina also makes them the ideal mount for endurance rides, since they are capable of covering great distances, in extremes of temperature, on the most modest of rations. One of the most celebrated of all endurance rides took place in 1935, when Akhal-Teke horses travelled from Ashkabad to Moscow (their journey included crossing the Karakum desert), completing a distance of 2,580 miles (4,152km) in 84 days.

Morgan

The American Morgan horse is highly unusual in that it can be traced back to just one stallion, the extraordinary little Justin Morgan, who stood a mere 14hh but who excelled in weight-pulling contests and races, both under saddle and in harness.

Justin Morgan was probably foaled in 1789 and was originally named Figure, later taking the name of his first recorded owner, Thomas Justin Morgan, who came from farming stock in Vermont but who was also a music teacher and church composer. How Justin Morgan was bred has never been satisfactorily resolved because of the lack of recorded evidence. Plausible claims have been made for Thoroughbred, Arab, Welsh Cob and Dutch ancestry. What is beyond dispute is that despite his small stature – he weighed no more than 850lb (386kg) – Justin Morgan proved himself a remarkably strong work horse, and he undoubtedly

worked extremely hard for a succession of owners. He was used for ploughing, as a harness horse and in woodland clearance and was never beaten in log-hauling matches against rivals weighing nearly half as much again.

He was, moreover, a wonderfully prepotent sire, passing on to his progeny all his own remarkable attributes of strength, endurance, speed and, not least, his gentle temperament. Three of his sons were to have a particular influence on

the development of the breed of which he was the founder: Sherman Morgan, foaled around 1808, Woodbury Morgan (1816) and Bulrush Morgan (1812). The Sherman Morgan line was noted for its excellent harness horses and had an important influence on the foundation of other breeds in the US: the Quarter Horse, Saddlebred, Standardbred and Tennessee Walker. The Woodbury Morgans were much in demand as saddle and parade

LEFT
The top line of the Morgan is distinctive. The gentle curve from the poll to the back gives the impression of the neck sitting on top of the withers rather than in front of them.

BREED DESCRIPTION

Height 14.1 – 15.2hh with some individuals over or under.

Colour Bay, chestnut, brown or black. No white markings permitted above the knee or hock, except on the face.

Conformation Expressive head, with straight or slightly dished profile, broad forehead, large eyes and short, alert ears; slightly arched neck; sloping shoulders and well-defined withers; compact, deep body, with short back, well-sprung ribs, broad loins and deep flank; well-muscled hindquarters with high-set tail; straight, sound legs, with short cannons, flat bone and sufficiently long, sloping pasterns to provide light, springy step; good, sound feet with dense horn; full, soft mane and tail.

horses, while the Bulrush Morgans were noted for their trotting speed.

Like so many other breeds, the Morgan horse went into decline with the coming of motorized transport, but thanks to the efforts of enthusiastic members of the Morgan Horse Club, founded in 1909, the breed survived. Today there is a thriving population of Morgan horses in the United States plus recognized breed clubs in Canada, Britain, Australia, Spain, New Zealand, Germany, Italy and Sweden. The Morgan is kept as a show horse and is also to be seen competing in a variety of spheres, such as cutting horse, stock horse and reining horse classes, hunter-jumper division, dressage and roadster and carriage driving competitions.

INTERESTING FACTS

A Morgan horse named Comanche, the mount of Captain Myles Keogh, was the only non-Indian survivor of the Battle of the Little Big Horn in 1876. He recovered from his many wounds and lived to the ripe old age of 29.

◾ **ABOVE**
The versatile Morgan horse is equally at home in harness and under saddle.

◾ **LEFT**
Morgan horses are well up to carrying the weight of adult riders. The action is straight and springy.

Quarter Horse

The Quarter Horse, as its name implies, excels at racing over a short distance – a quarter of a mile to be precise. It traces back to the horses taken to America by the Spanish Conquistadores. During the seventeenth and eighteenth centuries the waves of English settlers in the eastern states used the local Spanish-based stock to cross with their own, imported horses to produce a good, all-round work horse, suitable for every type of ridden work, for tilling the land and for work in harness. Tough and stocky, these horses became the settlers' "right-hand men". Spreading westward, they became indispensable during the great days of cattle herding when the chief requirement was for a totally dependable mount, one which was athletic and fearless working among cattle. In time these horses developed an innate "cow sense" and could anticipate the movements of a steer, stopping and turning at breakneck speed.

It was the Englishman's growing enthusiasm for racing which led to these all-purpose horses being raced in impromptu contests: on the road, in a clearing, anywhere where a couple of

■ ABOVE LEFT
The head of the Quarter Horse is short and wide with large, intelligent eyes, alert ears and a small muzzle.

■ ABOVE RIGHT
The chest is broad and deep, and the forelegs wide set. The muscling on the insides of the forearms gives the appearance of a well-defined inverted V.

■ RIGHT
The breed is noted for its strong, close-coupled back and deep girth. Well-muscled hindquarters and strong, low-set hocks give the horse its tremendous acceleration.

BREED DESCRIPTION

Height 14.3 – 16hh for mature stallions and mares.

Colour Any solid colour.

Conformation Short, wide head, with small muzzle, large, wide-set, intelligent eyes and medium-length, alert ears; fairly long, flexible neck; sloping shoulders and well-defined withers; compact body with broad chest, deep girth, short back, well-sprung ribs and powerful loins; broad, deep, heavy and well-muscled hindquarters with long, gently sloped croup; good limbs, with short cannons, broad, flat, low-set hocks, muscular thighs and gaskins and medium-length pasterns; oblong feet with deep, open heels.

▌ ABOVE
Quarter Horses have an innate "cow sense" and are able to anticipate the movements of a steer.

horses could be galloped upsides for a few hundred yards. The Quarter Horse, as it was dubbed, developed immensely powerful hindquarters, which could propel it into a flat-out gallop virtually from a standing start, and the speed to sprint over short distances. Eventually, however, as Thoroughbred racing became established, interest in Quarter Horse racing dwindled. Still later, when mechanization brought about a lessening of the horse's importance in ranching, the Quarter Horse, in common with riding horses all over the world, became a leisure riding horse.

Today the Quarter Horse enjoys great popularity in Western-style competitions such as barrel racing, in rodeos and, once again, in racing over short distances. Thanks to a revival of interest in the latter sport, Quarter Horses now compete on proper tracks for big purses.

INTERESTING FACTS

The American Quarter Horse Association was formed in 1940. Its registry is now the largest of any breed in the world, with more than two million horses listed.

▌ BELOW LEFT
The Quarter Horse makes an ideal mount for traditional Western sports.

▌ BELOW RIGHT
The breed is well known for its pleasant disposition and gentleness and as a result is used in a wide variety of activities.

Stop big lick!

Saddlebred

Formerly known as the Kentucky Saddler, the elegant Saddlebred was developed by the early nineteenth-century settlers in the southern states of North America. To meet their requirements for a quality utility horse, the plantation owners interbred horses of various kinds, including the Narragansett Pacer (a speedy strain of pacing horse from Rhode Island) and the Thoroughbred. The end result was a good-looking animal who gave an exceptionally comfortable ride – essential for long hours spent in the saddle on crop-inspection tours – but was equally well suited to pulling a carriage. In 1891 a group of leading breeders established the American Saddle Horse Breeders' Association and a Saddle Horse Registry was set up.

Blessed with the most amiable disposition, intelligence, speed and natural balance, the Saddlebred could (and still can) be used for all manner of different purposes, including working with cattle. Not surprisingly it has made the transition from work horse to pleasure

BREED DESCRIPTION

Height 15 – 17hh; average about 15.3hh.

Colour Usually chestnut, bay, brown, black or grey; also palomino, spotted and occasionally roan.

Conformation Well-shaped head with large eyes set well apart, small, alert ears and wide nostrils; long, arched neck; sloping shoulders with sharp withers; short, strong back; well-muscled hindquarters with level croup and high-set tail; straight, strong limbs with long, sloping pasterns; good, sound hooves, open at the heels.

Poor Saddlebreds

big lick puts gasoline and chains that hurt the horse to make them more fancy

■ TOP
Everything about the Saddlebred's head suggests quality, refinement and intelligence. The neck is always long and elegantly arched.

■ LEFT
The Saddlebred's top line is distinctive: the croup is long and level, the back short and the well-defined withers higher than in most other light breeds.

■ LEFT
Long, well-sloped pasterns contribute to the comfortable paces for which the breed is famous.

■ BELOW
As well as being popular riding horses, Saddlebreds go equally well in harness. The peculiar tail carriage is not natural, being achieved through an operation and maintained by keeping the tail in a device known as a tail set when the horse is stabled.

horse with no difficulty whatsoever and can be seen today competing in show classes under saddle and in harness.

In the show ring, ridden Saddlebreds are classified either as three-gaited or five-gaited. The three-gaited horses are shown at walk, trot and canter. The walk is springy, the trot has high action and the canter is slow, smooth and rhythmic. The five-gaited horses show these three paces plus two others: the slow gait and the rack. The slow gait is a high-stepping, four-beat gait executed in a slow, restrained manner. The rack is a fast, flashy, four-beat gait in which each foot strikes the ground at equal intervals and which is free from any lateral movement or pacing. The practice of growing the feet unnaturally long (to enhance the action), and operating on the tail to make it unnaturally high set, developed for the show ring.

Outside the artificial confines of the show ring, in its handsome natural state, the Saddlebred makes an excellent all-round riding horse – easy to train, fast, possessing great stamina and having a good jump, too.

INTERESTING FACTS

In their natural state the Saddlebred's strong hooves are well formed. For showing purposes they are grown to an unnatural length and shod with heavy shoes.

Standardbred

The American Standardbred is to harness racing what the English Thoroughbred is to flat racing and steeplechasing. During the past century or more, every country where harness racing flourishes has imported Standardbred horses to upgrade its own trotters and pacers.

BREED DESCRIPTION

Height 14 – 16hh.

Colour All solid colours, predominantly bay, brown, black and chestnut.

Conformation The Standardbred is a powerfully built horse, of rather less quality and refinement than the Thoroughbred and somewhat longer in the body and shorter in the leg. The shoulders are long and sloping and the croup invariably high.

I OPPOSITE PAGE
The gaits are so inherent that Standardbreds often show a marked preference for the trot (shown here) or the pace over the gallop, even when they are at liberty.

Strangely enough the foundation sire of the Standardbred was a horse who only ever raced at the gallop: the English Thoroughbred, Messenger. A grey tracing back to the Darley Arabian, Messenger was foaled in 1780 and raced on the flat for three seasons, winning eight of his fourteen starts. Exported to Philadelphia in May 1788, he stood at stud in America for twenty years, covering mainly Thoroughbred mares to start with then, after racing was suppressed in New York, all types of non-Thoroughbreds. Some of his descendants became fine flat

I ABOVE
The head of the Standardbred is not exactly refined but the overall aspect is workmanlike and the expression sensible.

I LEFT
In comparison with that other great racehorse, the Thoroughbred, the breed is rather long in the back and short in the leg. The shoulders are invariably long and well sloped, giving the horse the necessary freedom of movement.

INTERESTING FACTS

One of the greatest Standardbred trotters of all time, and the horse who did much to revive waning interest in harness racing in the 1930s, was the flying grey, Greyhound, who in 1938 trotted the mile in 1:55.25, a record that stood for 31 years. The mobile starting gate, introduced in 1946, eliminated time-wasting starts and together with greatly improved racing surfaces has contributed to the recording of increasingly faster times by both trotters and pacers.

racehorses but it was his ability to throw good trotting stock (not so much his immediate progeny as their descendants) that earned him lasting fame. His great grandson, Hambletonian, became a prolific sire of trotters and Hambletonian's four sons, George Wilkes, Dictator, Happy Medium and Electioneer, founded the sire lines responsible for virtually all harness racehorses in the USA today. Hambletonian was out of the Charles Kent Mare, who was inbred to Messenger, and descended, through her sire, Bellfounder, from the famous Norfolk Trotter, Old Shales.

In addition to the dominant Messenger line, two other important influences on

the early development of the Standardbred were the Clays (descendants of a Barb stallion imported from Tripoli in 1820) and the Morgan horse. Neither produced important families within the breed but both are believed to have helped establish its characteristic gait.

The first register of trotters was published in 1871 and the term "Standardbred" was introduced eight years later when a set of qualifications was drawn up for the admission of horses into the register. The original "standard", from which the breed takes its name, was judged to be the ability of a horse to cover a mile (1.6km) in 2 minutes 30 seconds (as trotters and pacers improved, this time

had to be reduced). Standardbreds race either at the pace (a lateral gait) or the trot (a diagonal pace). Up until the last couple of decades of the nineteenth century, trotters were more popular than the marginally faster pacers, but this is not so today.

■ ABOVE
Although the pace is one of the breed's natural gaits it is usual for pacing racehorses to wear hobbles to encourage them to maintain the lateral movement.

■ LEFT
Racing harness includes many items not generally seen in other horse sports. The shadow rolls on this horse's bridle are designed to prevent him from seeing and taking fright at shadows or "foreign objects" on the ground.

Missouri Fox Trotter

Although a stud book for the Missouri Fox Trotting Horse was not opened until 1948, the breed began to evolve in the early part of the nineteenth century. Settlers travelling westwards across the Mississippi river from Kentucky, Tennessee and Virginia took with them a variety of horses, including Thoroughbreds, eastern-bred stock and Morgans, and then interbred them to produce a horse suited to the conditions of their new home in the Ozark Hills region of Missouri.

The chief requirement, especially of doctors, sheriffs, stock raisers and the like, was for a horse that could be ridden for long periods, often over rough terrain, with a minimum of fatigue either to horse or rider. The answer was found in the gait known as the fox trot, in which the horse walks with its forelegs but trots behind. The Fox Trotter does not put its hindfeet down with the jarring action characteristic of the

BREED DESCRIPTION

Height 14 – 16hh.

Colour Any. Most commonly sorrel and chestnut sorrel with white markings.

Conformation Neat, clean, intelligent head with pointed, well-shaped ears, large, bright eyes and a tapered muzzle; graceful neck, in proportion to length of body; well-sloped, muscular shoulders; deep, strong body with deep, full chest and short, strong back; strong, muscular limbs; strong, well-made feet.

▌ ABOVE
This neat, intelligent looking head, with its bright eyes and well-shaped ears, is typical of the Missouri Fox Trotter.

▌ RIGHT
The body is deep, the back short and the overall impression one of compactness. Well-sloped shoulders ensure good riding action.

The legendary comfort experienced when riding a Fox Trotter comes from the unusual action of the hindfeet, which slide forward under the horse as he puts them down, rather than hitting the ground with a jarring action.

INTERESTING FACTS

In the fox trot the horse's hindfeet disfigure the tracks of the forefeet, that is the hindfeet touch the front tracks and slide forward. The horse should travel in a collected manner, with animation, rhythm and style. The horse's tail is slightly elevated and moves in a bobbing rhythm with the gait. The flat-foot walk should also be performed with style and animation. It is an animated four-beat gait in which the horse overstrides its front track with the hindfeet. The typical canter of the Fox Trotter is collected, with the head and tail slightly elevated.

normal trot, but slides them along under him. The result is a smooth, comfortable gait at which the horse can travel for extended periods without tiring. The ability to walk in front and trot behind is inherited but it can also be enhanced with training. The overall quality of the Fox

show classes in which it is judged 40 per cent for the fox trot, 20 per cent for the flat foot walk, 20 per cent for the canter and 20 per cent for conformation, the only exceptions being two-year-olds, who are judged 50 per cent for fox trot, 25 per cent for walk and 25 per cent for conformation.

▌ BELOW LEFT
Originally bred as a means of transport, the present-day Fox Trotter is well suited to modern leisure riding. It is renowned for its sure-footedness.

▌ BELOW
Unlike the Saddlebred and the Tennessee Walking Horse, the Missouri Fox Trotter is shown with normal-length feet. Artificial appliances such as weights and tail sets are forbidden.

Trotter was improved over the years through infusions of Saddlebred and Tennessee Walker blood and today the breed is noted for its compact, muscular build and its sure-footedness.

Having become obsolete as a means of transport, the Fox Trotter is now used as a pleasure horse, being ideally suited to trail (long-distance) riding. It is also ridden in

Tennessee Walking Horse

The Tennessee Walking Horse traces back to the Narragansett Pacer and, like the Saddlebred and the Missouri Fox Trotter, it was developed as an exceptionally comfortable riding horse with gaits not found in other breeds. Originally known as the Southern Plantation Walking Horse or Tennessee Pacer, it was an invaluable mode of transport for planters carrying out crop inspections, being fast, robust, comfortable under saddle and having a most tractable temperament.

The foundation sire was a horse named Black Allan, who arrived in Tennessee in

■ LEFT
The Tennessee Walking Horse is customarily ridden in a plain bit with long shanks and on a single rein which is held with a light hand and flexed wrist.

■ BELOW
The Walking Horse has the substance of the Standardbred and the style of the Saddlebred which are two of the breeds on which it is based.

1903. Black Allan's sire came from a line of Standardbred trotters, while his dam was a Morgan. Black Allan was crossed with the Tennessee Pacers of the time to produce the forerunners of the modern Walking Horse. Saddlebred blood was also introduced, the most important influence being that of Giovanni, who in 1914 was brought from Kentucky to stand at stud in Tennessee. By adding Saddlebred blood, breeders succeeded in producing a better quality, more refined, animal. Today's Walking Horse, which might be decribed as a somewhat more powerful version of

BREED DESCRIPTION

Height Average 15 .2hh.

Colour Any. Black and solid colours are most popular.

Conformation Intelligent but rather plain head; strong, arched neck; well-sloped shoulders; powerful body with broad chest; strong hindquarters; clean, hard limbs.

the Saddlebred, is therefore an amalgam of Thoroughbred, Standardbred, Morgan and Saddlebred blood. The Tennessee Walking Horse Breeders' Association was formed in Lewisburg, Tennessee, in 1935 and the Walking Horse was finally recognized as a breed in 1947.

Walking horses are fine all-round riding horses, their inherently kind nature making them especially suitable for novice riders. They are also popular horses in the show ring.

INTERESTING FACTS

The Tennessee Walking Horse's distinctive gaits – the flat-foot walk, the running walk and the canter – are inherited. Small foals can be seen performing the running walk beside their dams. Both walks are a loose, four-beat gait, with high action in front. As it moves, the horse nods its head in rhythm with the rise and fall of the hoofs, and the hindfeet overstride the tracks left by the front feet. The flat-foot walk should be loose, bold and square with plenty of shoulder motion. There should be a noticeable difference in the tempo between the two walks. The canter has a distinctive "rocking chair" motion.

LEFT
The breed's unique gaits are inherited – young foals are seen to "walk" alongside their mothers with the ease of older horses – but are encouraged with artificial aids applied to the forefeet.

FAR LEFT
An impressive collection of Walking Horse trophies won in America, where the breed is a popular showring attraction.

BELOW
The exaggerated outline of the show horse is produced in part by the extra-long forefeet. The rider sits way behind the normal saddle position (on what is generally held to be the weakest part of the horse's back).

Mustang

Mustangs, the "wild" horses of North America, are descended from the horses taken to the New World by the sixteenth-century Conquistadores. As Spanish colonizers began moving north from Mexico into what is now Texas, so the Indian tribes with whom they came into contact began to have their first experience of horses. Initially, the Indians were inclined to kill and eat any horses they captured from the settlers. In time, however, as they began to realize the value of the horse as a means of transport, they learnt how to handle and ride them.

By the second half of the seventeenth century, some tribes were taking horses from the Spaniards and using them in mounted raids against the newcomers – during which they would acquire more horses. So began the gradual spread of the horse to other tribes (either by trading or by theft) and the movement of the horse

 LEFT
This Mustang shows unmistakable signs of its Spanish ancestry in its attractive head and luxurious growth of silky mane.

BREED DESCRIPTION

Height 13.2 – 15hh.

Colour Any.

Conformation Because of its mixed ancestry (the original Spanish stock was progressively diluted as a wide variety of settlers' horses, who either became lost or were abandoned, joined and interbred with the wild herds) there is a good deal of variation. The best are sturdily built with strong, clean limbs and feet.

northwards. Many of the horses who subsequently ran "wild" would have done so after getting loose during skirmishes between Indians and Spaniards. Others, perhaps those who were lame or needed resting, were probably turned loose, their owners intending to round them up later. Some domestic horses put out to graze on the range simply wandered off. Gradually these horses joined together to form feral

herds, which flourished in the wide open spaces of the Great Plains. By the late eighteenth and early nineteenth centuries there were huge numbers of "wild" horses grazing the plains – one authority estimates the number to have been as high as two million.

The turning point for the Mustang, as these feral horses became known, was the westward spread of civilization. Many were

 RIGHT
Because of its chequered history, Mustang conformation is very variable. Not all horses are as sturdily built as this one.

▌ LEFT
Centuries of living in a feral state led to the
development of a tough, enduring type of animal.

INTERESTING FACTS

The term mustang probably comes from the
Spanish word *mesteno*, from *mesta*, meaning
an association of graziers or stock raisers. In
thirteenth-century Spain *mestas* were
organizations of sheep owners. Stray sheep
were called *mestenos*, meaning "belonging to
the *mesta*". Some etymologists think that
mustang comes from the word *mestengo*, a
later form of *mostrenco*, from the verb
mostrar, to show or exhibit. Stray sheep,
sometimes referred to as *mostrencos*, were
shown in public to give the owner the chance
to claim them. But according to the wild-
horse authority J. Frank Dobie, English-
speaking people in the American south-west
did not know the word *mostrenco*. Dobie
dates the introduction of the term Mustang
to the early nineteenth century.

killed, others were rounded up for use as
draught animals, some were used for
cross-breeding. Large numbers were used
as army remounts in the Boer War. During
the twentieth century still more have been
killed for the meat and pet food trades.

Public pressure led to the introduction,
in 1971, of an act giving protection to wild
horses in the United States and there are
several ranges where they still live, albeit
in much reduced numbers. Domesticated
Mustangs often make good riding horses.
Because of their inherent toughness, they
are well suited to endurance rides.

▌ LEFT
A fine stamp of Mustang which looks well under
saddle. The majority of domesticated Mustangs
make good all-round riding horses.

▌ RIGHT
Decorated in
traditional style, these
horses reflect their
links with the Indian
tribes who came to rely
on the horses first
introduced into
America by the
Conquistadores.

Australian Stock Horse

Horses were not indigenous to Australia and the modern Stock Horse is descended from the first imported animals, shipped over in small numbers from South Africa during the latter part of the eighteenth century. The precise breeding of these early imports is not known but they were probably of mainly Arab and Barb blood. It was not long before regular voyages began between Europe and Australia, each ship with its quota of horses aboard, and so Australia's equine population steadily grew.

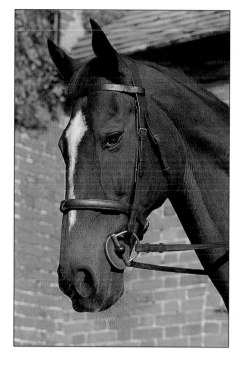

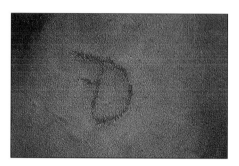

BREED DESCRIPTION

Height 15 – 16.3hh.

Colour Any solid colour.

Conformation There is considerable variation, but the best types are similar to the Thoroughbred, with particularly good sound limbs and feet.

Tough horses were needed to help settlers explore their rugged new home and, not surprisingly, Thoroughbreds and Arabs were the most popular imports. Thoroughbreds were required, too, to satisfy the growing interest of the settlers in racing, a sport which rapidly gained popularity from the early years of the nineteenth century onwards.

The horse which evolved for everyday use was a tough all-rounder: hardy, reliable, of good temperament, able to work in harness or under saddle, to plough the land, clear timber, and herd cattle and sheep. Until 1971, when the term Stock Horse was introduced, it was known as the "Waler" (after New South Wales). Walers were renowned for their stamina, courage and soundness and were accordingly highly prized by the cavalry.

The present-day Stock Horse is the descendant of the Waler. It has almost certainly been influenced by a number of breeds other than the Thoroughbred and Arab – Quarter Horses, various ponies and heavy breeds such as the Clydesdale and Suffolk Punch were all imported into Australia over the years and some out-crosses would have been made – but the Stock Horse is essentially a quality riding horse. Still in demand for cattle herding, at which it excels, it can also be seen taking part in rodeos and is suitable for general riding purposes, including competitive sports.

INTERESTING FACTS

Regal Realm is one of a long line of Australian Stock Horses to compete successfully at the highest level. Ridden by Lucinda Green he won the individual gold medal at the World Three-Day Event Championships in 1982, helping Britain to take the team title. The following year he was runner-up in the European Championships, winning a team silver medal. At the Los Angeles Olympic Games in 1984 he won another team silver and finished in sixth place individually. A year later he was a member of the victorious British team in the European Championships. When he retired from international competition he returned to his native land.

▌ OPPOSITE ABOVE LEFT
The head resembles that of the Thoroughbred, which is one of the major influences in the development of the Australian Stock Horse.

▌ OPPOSITE ABOVE RIGHT
It is usual to brand Stock Horses for identification purposes. This brand is on the horse's shoulder.

▌ OPPOSITE BELOW
Many Stock Horses show the refinement and good overall conformation of the Thoroughbred. They have as a result produced some good sports horses.

▌ LEFT
There is as yet no set type within the breed. This striking-looking horse shows unmistakable signs of his eastern ancestry.

▌ BELOW
The breed was and still is a cattle-herding horse par excellence: tough, enduring, sound and good-natured.

Criollo

A descendant of the horses taken to South America by the sixteenth-century Spanish Conquistadores, the Criollo comes from Argentina and is one of the toughest breeds of horse in the world. Its hardiness is the result of many years of natural selection. Some of the Spanish horses and their descendants formed feral herds on the pampas, where the extremes of climate – intensely dry, hot summers and severe winters – would have proved intolerable to all but the sturdiest individuals. Those that survived adapted to their harsh environment remarkably well, no doubt helped by the fact that they were descended from Andalusian and Barb horses, both breeds noted for their endurance. The Criollo, as it became known, even developed a coat colour – Criollos are predominantly dun – which helped render it inconspicuous against

BREED DESCRIPTION

Height Around 14 – 15hh.

Colour Usually dun with dark points and often with a dorsal stripe.

Conformation Medium-sized head, with wide-set eyes and alert ears; muscular neck; short, deep body with well-sprung ribs; short, strong limbs with plenty of bone and good, sound feet.

the dry pastureland of its habitat.

The Criollo became the favoured mount of the gauchos, the cowboys of the pampas, and an indispensable riding and packhorse for settlers in the huge and frequently inhospitable countries of South America. It can be found throughout the continent and although there are some variations, the result of adaptation to differences in habitat and climate, wherever it is bred it retains its basic qualities of stamina and soundness. Crossed with the Thoroughbred, the Criollo produces a fine polo pony, the Thoroughbred blood providing the extra speed required in the modern game.

INTERESTING FACTS

The most famous example of the Criollo's extraordinary powers of endurance was "Tschiffely's Ride", a journey undertaken by the Swiss-born traveller and writer Aimé Felix Tschiffely (1895–1954). In 1925, together with two Criollos – the 16-year-old Mancha, and the 15-year-old Gata – Tschiffely set off from Buenos Aires to ride to Washington D.C. in the United States. Alternately riding one horse and leading the other as a packhorse, he completed the journey, over some of the most arduous terrain in the world, in two and a half years. The horses were then shipped back to South America, where they spent their retirement, Gata living to the age of 36 and Mancha to 40.

Peruvian Paso

The Paso (meaning "step") is another breed which owes its origins to the Barb and Andalusian horses introduced to South America by the Spaniards. The first horses to arrive in Peru were taken there in 1532 by Francisco Pizarro (c.1478–1541).

The Paso's characteristic lateral gait is thought to have been inherited from the Spanish "jennet", which was a riding horse akin to the old English ambler. The lateral movement has been preserved down the centuries; the Paso usually demonstrates a preference for it over the canter. The paso is unlike any other lateral gait in that the horse's forelegs arc out to the side as he moves. With his hindlegs he takes long, straight strides, carrying his hindquarters

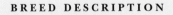

BREED DESCRIPTION

Height 14 – 15.2hh.

Colour Any, but predominantly bay and chestnut.

Conformation Intelligent looking head; fairly short, muscular neck; strong shoulders; strong body with broad, deep chest; strong, rounded hindquarters; short, strong limbs and excellent feet.

low, with his hocks well under him. This combination of flowing foreleg movement and powerfully driving hindlegs gives a particularly smooth ride. The Paso is said to be able to reach speeds of up to 15mph (24kph) and to maintain the lateral gait over rough terrain for extended periods without tiring.

Fairly small and stockily built, the Paso is noted for its sure-footedness, its ability to thrive on meagre rations and its kind nature. It makes an ideal ranch and long-distance riding horse.

▌ **RIGHT**
Horse and rider make an attractive, workmanlike picture in their traditional Peruvian tack and costume. The Paso is up to carrying a good deal of weight.

▌ **ABOVE**
Compact and well-muscled, with powerful hindquarters and short, strong limbs, the Peruvian Paso is a tremendously strong individual.

▌ **LEFT**
The Paso's long silky mane (and tail) is reminiscent of that of its Spanish ancestors, introduced into South America during the sixteenth century.

INTERESTING FACTS

The Peruvian Paso is not the only horse to show a natural preference for a lateral gait but the curious outward arcing of the forelegs, which move rather like the arms of a swimmer, is unique to the breed.

Ponies

Broadly speaking a pony is a small horse, "small" usually meaning no higher at the withers than about 14.2hh (a hand is 4 inches). However, not all small horses can be classified as ponies. Arab horses, for example, often stand below 15hh but they are very much horses, with the proportions and characteristics of the horse. An unusually small Thoroughbred is certainly not a pony and the remarkable little Caspian, although it is classified as a pony, actually resembles a miniature horse.

True ponies have very distinct pony characteristics, which include a proportionately short length of leg in relationship to the depth of the body. True ponies are perhaps best exemplified by the Mountain and Moorland breeds of Britain and Ireland, remarkable animals which have existed in the comparative isolation of their island home for thousands of years. These ponies, which are now divided into nine distinct breeds, are possessed of extraordinary strength in relation to their size. Fashioned by a harsh environment, they are tough, sure-footed, able to exist on minimum rations and have an inherent sagacity often lacking in their larger cousins.

Haflinger

Austria's attractive Haflinger pony is named after the village of Hafling in the southern Tirol, the region where it was first bred hundreds of years ago. Its ancestors were indigenous mountain

BREED DESCRIPTION

Height Around 14hh.

Colour Chestnut with flaxen mane and tail.

Conformation Intelligent looking head, with large eyes, small ears and slightly dished profile; sloping shoulders; strong, deep body with fairly long back and muscular loins; powerful hindquarters; strong limbs and excellent feet.

■ PREVIOUS PAGE OPPOSITE
Exmoor ponies.

■ PREVIOUS PAGE
A Norwegian Fjord pony.

■ LEFT
The "Hungarian Post" – Haflinger style! The breed combines strength with very active paces and can be trained to perform in a wide range of equestrian activities.

■ BELOW LEFT
Haflingers are true all-rounders, equally adept at work in harness and under saddle. This handsome team was photographed in Switzerland.

■ BELOW
The Haflinger's good temperament is easily discerned in this attractive head, with its large, kind eyes and alert expression.

horses and ponies which were upgraded with Arabian blood. All modern Haflingers trace back to a half-bred horse named El Bedavi XXII – who was bred in Austria and was a great grandson of the Arabian stallion, El Bedavi – and to El Bedavi XXII's son, Folie.

Over the years inbreeding has resulted in a pony of very definite type: small, but powerfully built, always chestnut in colour, hardy and sure-footed as befits a mountain pony, and with the active paces of its Arab forebears.

With its amenable nature, the Haflinger makes an excellent all-round riding and driving pony. Before mechanization it was in great demand for agricultural work and as a pack-pony. Nowadays many Haflingers are used for leisure riding. The breed has been exported to a number of countries, and is especially popular in Germany and Switzerland. It is noted for its longevity.

INTERESTING FACTS

Haflingers which are entered in the breed's stud book are traditionally branded. The brand mark is the alpine flower, the edelweiss, at the centre of which is placed the letter "H".

Sorraia

Formerly used for farm work and general riding purposes, the primitive looking Sorraia survives today mainly in small feral groups. Its homeland is in Portugal in the region between the rivers Sor and Raia, tributaries of the Sorraia, which flows into the Tagus estuary from the south.

The Sorraia pony is believed to be descended from the Asian Wild Horse and the Tarpan. It bears a remarkable likeness to the latter, with its small stature and large head. The Sorraia's colouring, predominantly dun, often with an eel-stripe and zebra markings on the legs, is also typical of the primitive equine type.

The Sorraia does not have the best conformation in the world. It is, however, an extremely tough individual, able to exist on poor forage and to withstand extremes of climate. The shoulders tend to be upright, the hindquarters weak and the limbs rather long and lacking in bone, though the feet are hard and sound.

■ **LEFT**
Dun is the predominant colour of the Sorraia, Portugal's small, semi-feral pony. The breed is of ancient origin and is exceptionally hardy.

■ **BELOW**
In build and overall outline the Sorraia is not unlike the primitive Tarpan. Some selective breeding is carried out in order to preserve the original form.

BREED DESCRIPTION

Height 12 – 13hh.

Colour Predominantly dun, with black eel-stripe down the centre of the back and frequently with zebra markings on the legs and occasionally on the body; also grey.

Conformation Large, primitive looking head with convex profile; straight shoulders; poor hindquarters with low-set tail; long limbs, lacking in bone.

INTERESTING FACTS

The Sorraia is believed to be related to the Garrano, the pony of northern Portugal. The Garrano shows more quality than the Sorraia, the result of infusions of Arab blood. Although small, the Garrano is inherently hardy, and has been used for all types of farm work, as a pack-pony and for hauling timber.

Exmoor

The Exmoor is the oldest of Britain's Mountain and Moorland breeds and one of the oldest equine breeds in the world. This attractive pony has inhabited the wild moorland area of west Somerset and north Devon in the south-west of England for many centuries. Ponies of Exmoor type were certainly known during Roman times and may well have existed as far back as the Bronze Age, when they would have been used for pulling chariots. Mention is made of Exmoor ponies and their owners in the Domesday Book of 1085.

The remoteness of its habitat has meant that the Exmoor pony has been subjected to very little in the way of

"improvement" through the introduction of outside blood. The rigours of life on the moor have produced a tremendously hardy pony, strong enough to carry an adult rider in spite of the fact that the ponies stand no higher than 12.3hh.

The Exmoor Pony Society was founded in 1921 to improve and encourage the breeding of Exmoor ponies of the

traditional moorland type. By carrying out rigorous inspections, it ensures that no pony lacking true Exmoor type is registered as a pure-bred. When ponies are passed for registration, they are branded on the shoulder with the

---

BREED DESCRIPTION

Height Stallions and geldings not exceeding 12.3hh. Mares not exceeding 12.2hh.

Colour Bay, brown or dun with black points. No white markings anywhere.

Conformation Clean-cut face with wide forehead, large, prominent eyes, wide nostrils and clean throat; good length of rein; well laid-back shoulders; strong body with deep, wide chest, well-sprung ribs and broad, level back; clean, short limbs and neat, hard feet.

▍ TOP
The Exmoor's attractive head, notable for its large eyes, small, mobile ears and intelligent expression, is full of true pony character.

▍ RIGHT
The Exmoor is a fine stamp of pony: hard and strong, vigorous, alert and symmetrical in appearance. Its general poise indicates its good natural balance.

Society's star brand. Beneath this the pony's herd number appears, while on the nearside hindquarter there is the pony's own number within that herd.

Herds of ponies still run "wild" on the moor, although they are rounded up annually for inspection. The Exmoor's robust build and constitution make it an excellent riding pony and they are also used in the sport of driving.

■ ABOVE
Correctly handled and schooled, the Exmoor, for all its great strength, makes a good riding pony for a small child.

INTERESTING FACTS

The most instantly recognizable features of the Exmoor are its mealy coloured muzzle and its large, prominent eyes. The latter are termed "toad" eyes because of their heavy top lids. The eyebrows are surrounded by light, buff-coloured hair.

■ LEFT
The breed's inherent athleticism makes it a good all-round performance pony for an older child.

Dartmoor

BREED DESCRIPTION

Height Not exceeding 12.2hh.

Colour Bay, black or brown preferred, but no colours are barred except skewbald and piebald. Excessive white markings discouraged.

Conformation Small, well set-on head with small, alert ears; strong, medium length neck, not too heavy, stallions to have a moderate crest; strong back and loins; strong, muscular hindquarters with full, high-set tail; hard, well-shaped feet.

Unlike its neighbour, the Exmoor, the Dartmoor Pony has been influenced by a number of breeds over the many centuries during which ponies have run free on the high moorland of Devon, in south-west England. Ponies are thought to have lived on the moor during Saxon times. Later the important trade route which existed between Exeter and Plymouth would have been travelled by horses of many different types, some of which would almost certainly have had an influence on the native stock. Arabs and Barbs, brought back by Crusaders, are also believed to have found their way onto the moor.

Climate and the hardships of existing in such a wild region would have ensured

that the animals roaming the moors achieved a certain degree of uniformity, particularly with regard to size. During the Industrial Revolution the requirements of the mining industry prompted a new development: the crossing of Dartmoor Ponies with the much smaller Shetland, in order to produce animals suited to working underground. This proved to be a

highly retrograde step as far as the Dartmoor Pony was concerned. The type of riding-quality pony that had evolved began to deteriorate. In order to set matters right, new blood had to be introduced, including Welsh Mountain Pony, Polo Pony and Hackney.

The first stud book for Dartmoors was opened in 1899 and the height limits for

❚ LEFT
Strength and active paces make the Dartmoor a good harness pony.

INTERESTING FACTS

There was a steady decline in the numbers of ponies of true Dartmoor type after World War II and many of those found on the moor were only poor quality cross-breds. However, in 1988 the Dartmoor Pony Society Moor Scheme was set up in order to encourage farmers with unregistered pure-bred type ponies to offer them for registration and to provide them with the services of pedigree stallions. The aim is to establish a pool of pure-bred ponies – hardy enough to thrive on the moor – to which breeders can then go for true native pony characteristics. Suitable mares from the moor are put in large enclosed areas known as newtakes together with a pedigree stallion. Their female progeny are inspected and those which pass muster are entered in a supplementary register of the stud book. In due course these ponies will also be mated to a fully registered stallion, and so on until their descendants, on inspection, can be admitted to the full stud book.

❚ RIGHT
Dartmoors have a calm temperament and make good mounts for children.

❚ OPPOSITE TOP
The Dartmoor's neat, well set-on head with its small, alert ears, shows true native pony character.

❚ OPPOSITE BOTTOM
The best examples of the breed combine quality with great hardiness.

❚ BELOW
Although Dartmoor ponies declined in number and quality after World War II, in recent times measures have been introduced to ensure the preservation of a pool of hardy pure-breds.

stallions was given as 14hh and for mares 13.2hh. It was more than twenty years before this was reduced to the present 12.2hh. Hackney blood was prominent in a number of the foundation stallions. However, the most influential sire of those early years was undoubtedly The Leat, who was by a pure-bred Arab (Dwarka, who stood 14.1hh) out of a Dartmoor mare. Standing 12.2hh, The Leat was a beautiful looking pony with excellent conformation. During his short stud career only a handful of his progeny were registered, but many of the best present-day ponies trace back to him.

At its best the Dartmoor is a hardy, quality riding pony with smooth, low, free action. Its sound constitution, intelligence and excellent, calm temperament, make it an ideal pony for a child.

Welsh Mountain

The rugged landscape of Wales is home to four distinct equine breeds: two ponies, designated Section A and Section B in the Welsh Pony and Cob Society Stud Book, and two cobs, designated Section C and Section D.

At the base of all Welsh breeding is the beautiful Welsh Mountain Pony, Section A, which has thrived for many centuries in the tough environment of its native land

▮ ABOVE
The eastern influence is clearly visible in the beautiful head, with its big eyes, wide nostrils and dished profile.

▮ LEFT
The Section B is larger than the Welsh Mountain Pony but the best examples have the same true pony character. The action is straight, quick and free.

▮ BELOW
Section A ponies like this one were used in the development of the Australian Pony, which is based on Welsh and Arab blood.

BREED DESCRIPTION

Height Not exceeding 12hh.

Colour Predominantly grey, though bay, chestnut and palomino occur and any solid colour is permitted.

Conformation Small, clean-cut head, tapering to the muzzle, with bold eyes, small, pointed ears and prominent, open nostrils; lengthy, well-carried neck; long, sloping shoulders; strong, muscular back with deep girth, well-sprung ribs and strong loins; lengthy, fine hindquarters with tail well set on and carried gaily; good, strong limbs, with long, strong forearm, well-developed knee, large, flat hocks and well-shaped feet, of dense, hard horn.

and is considered by many people to be the most beautiful of all ponies. The development of the breed is obscure, but it goes back at least to the times of the Romans, who crossed horses of eastern origin with the native Welsh stock. In more recent times, particularly during the eighteenth century, some Thoroughbred, Arab and Barb blood was introduced.

The modern Welsh Mountain Pony is courageous and spirited, yet kindly, and makes a superb child's riding pony. It is also an outstanding performer in the increasingly popular sport of carriage driving. It has evolved as a supremely hardy individual, able to endure harsh weather conditions and to thrive on sparse rations. It has been used to improve other breeds, including the New Forest, and also in the development of the British Riding Pony. The Welsh Mountain Pony is popular in many countries outside its native Wales. It has been exported to Europe, the United States, New Zealand and Australia.

INTERESTING FACTS

The Welsh Pony (Section B) is larger than the Mountain Pony, though it retains the true pony characteristics. Arab, small Thoroughbred and small Welsh Cob stallions were crossed with Mountain Pony mares to develop this quality riding pony, which stands up to 13.2hh. Formerly used for shepherding and hunting, Welsh Ponies are now much in demand as children's riding ponies.

New Forest

Wild horses are known to have existed in the New Forest, in southern England, as far back as the time of Canute (c. 995–1035). The exact origins of today's New Forest Pony are, however, unknown although it has certainly been influenced down the years by a variety of other breeds. During the eighteenth century the Thoroughbred stallion Marske, the sire of the great racehorse Eclipse, was used for a time to

BREED DESCRIPTION

Height 13.3 – 14.2hh.

Colour Any colour except skewbald, piebald, or blue-eyed cream.

Conformation Rather large head; fairly short neck; well-sloped shoulders; deep body; strong hindquarters; straight limbs with plenty of bone and good hard, round feet.

serve New Forest mares and in the mid-nineteenth century an Arab stallion belonging to Queen Victoria was allowed to run with the herds. Hackney blood was also introduced. While these infusions of outside blood added to the pony's size, they were detrimental when it came to the preservation of true pony substance and to rectify the situation, outcrosses were made to stallions of other native breeds, including Dales, Dartmoor, Exmoor, Fell, Highland and, later, Welsh Mountain.

Today's New Forest Ponies, like many Exmoor and Welsh Mountain Ponies, still roam freely in their native habitat. Life in the Forest can be hard, the food supply often meagre and low in quality. This tough environment has produced a hardy, sure-footed animal. The pony's action is free, active and straight and its good temperament makes it easy to train. As a result they make excellent all-round riding and driving ponies. They are popular not only in their native country but also in mainland Europe, North America, Australia and New Zealand.

INTERESTING FACTS

The ponies are owned by the New Forest Commoners, who carry out an annual "drift" or round-up in order to select those which are to be sold. The remaining breeding stock is then returned to the Forest.

▌ TOP
The best type of New Forest Pony is strongly built and possesses good, well-sloped riding shoulders, powerful hindquarters and strong, sound limbs

▌ ABOVE LEFT
The New Forest's head indicates the breed's typically calm, tractable temperament.

Dales

The Dales Pony comes from the Upper Dales (river valleys) of the eastern side of the Pennine Hills in northern England. It shares the same ancestors as its slightly larger neighbour, the Fell Pony, whose traditional home is on the western side of the Pennines. These ponies are believed to be descended from horses of the Roman period, when Friesians were introduced into northern England – this could have been the source of the Dales' predominantly black colouring. In more recent times various outcrosses are said to have been made, Norfolk Roadster among them. Some Welsh Cob blood was used during the nineteenth century and also Clydesdale. Despite the introduction of the latter, the Dales has retained its pony character, as can be seen in its neat head with its small, mobile ears.

The Dales is noted for its tremendously active paces and its great strength in relation to its size. At one time it played a vital part in lead mining, working both under- and overground, carrying loads of lead ore to the sea ports. It was also much

BREED DESCRIPTION

Height Not exceeding 14.2hh.

Colour Predominantly black, also bay, brown and, occasionally, grey.

Conformation Small, neat head, with wide forehead, bright eyes and small, erect ears; well-sloped shoulders; strong, deep body with short back, well-sprung ribs and strong loins; well-developed hindquarters; strong limbs with short straight cannons, good, clean joints and broad, very hard, well-shaped feet; fine, silky feather at the heel.

INTERESTING FACTS

Dales Ponies are inherently sure-footed. Their forebears are said to have been used by the Romans when constructing Hadrian's Wall in the inhospitable tract of country between the mouth of the River Tyne and the marshes of the Solway Firth in northern England.

used by the army. Stamina, courage and a docile temperament, coupled with its great strength and energy make the Dales a first-rate all-round riding and driving pony. It jumps, is intelligent, has a sensible, calm temperament and can carry an adult with ease.

▌ TOP
There have been native ponies on either side of the Pennines and in the Scottish borders for many centuries. They trace back in part to the Scottish Galloway although the Dales' black colouring probably comes from the influence of Friesian blood.

▌ LEFT
The breed is particularly renowned for its strong limbs, good bone and excellent feet.

Fell

Like its relative, the Dales, the Fell Pony is believed to be descended from the Friesian which was brought to northern England during Roman times. Down the centuries it, too, was almost certainly influenced by the now extinct Galloway, the mount of border reivers (raiders, particularly cattle thieves) who needed a strong, fast, sure-footed horse for their nefarious purposes.

BREED DESCRIPTION

Height Not exceeding 14hh.

Colour Black, brown, bay and grey, preferably with no white markings, though a star or a little white on the foot is allowed.

Conformation Small, well set-on head with broad forehead, bright, prominent eye, small, neat ears, large nostrils and fine throat and jaws; strong neck but not too heavy, giving a good length of rein; good, sloping shoulders; strong, deep body with muscular loins; strong hindquarters with well set-on tail; strong limbs with plenty of good flat bone below the knee and well-formed feet with characteristic blue horn.

INTERESTING FACTS

HRH The Duke of Edinburgh competes in trials with a team of HM The Queen's Fell Ponies. With their lively trot and great stamina they are well suited to the marathon phase, run over a distance of 16 miles.

The Fell has evolved as a somewhat smaller, lighter pony than the Dales (official recognition of a distinction between the two did not come until 1916, when the Dales Pony Improvement Society and the Fell Pony Society were formed). The Fell is, nevertheless, enormously strong and, like the Dales, was used as a pack-pony. During the eighteenth century it transported lead, coal and iron ore to the coast, carrying up to 16 stone (224lb/101kg) at a time in panniers. Some were used in pack-trains to carry produce such as wool as far as London.

The Fell is noted for its good paces, having a fast, active walk and a swift trot. Now that it is no longer in demand for pack work, shepherding and general farm work, it has become a popular all-round pleasure pony. It makes an excellent mount for trekking, goes superbly across country, both under saddle and in harness, and has the paces to do well in pure dressage.

▌ ABOVE
Fell ponies are native to the western side of the Pennines. They are slightly smaller than their near neighbours, the Dales, but have the same inherent toughness and active paces.

▌ BELOW
The Fell makes a first-class riding pony. These ponies, pictured at a breed.performance show, were competing in show jumping and mounted games as well as in show classes.

Highland

One of the strongest and heaviest of Britain's Mountain and Moorland breeds, the Highland Pony comes from the Highlands of Scotland and the islands off the west coast. Ponies are believed to have inhabited the region many thousands of years ago. The modern Highland Pony, sure-footed, hardy and long-lived, evolved as a result of various outcrosses, particularly Arab and Clydesdale. The Dukes of Atholl, influential breeders of Highland Ponies for several centuries, almost certainly introduced eastern blood as early as the sixteenth century.

Until fairly recently the breed was divided into two types: a more substantial mainland type, which stood up to 14.2hh, and the lighter, somewhat smaller Western Isles type. Although the Highland Pony Society, founded in 1923, no longer recognizes these distinctions, differences in type can still be discerned to some extent.

The Highland is a strong, sturdily built pony, a real all-round worker which in its time has carried men to war, been the mount of shepherds, worked in harness, hauled timber, taken deer-stalkers into the hills and carried the shot stags – weighing

BREED DESCRIPTION

Height 13 – 14.2hh.

Colour Various shades of dun, also grey, brown, black and occasionally bay and liver chestnut with silver mane and tail.

Conformation Well-carried head with broad forehead, alert, kindly eyes and wide nostrils; strong, arched neck with clean throat; well laid-back shoulders; compact body with deep chest and well-sprung ribs; powerful hindquarters with strong, well-developed thigh and second thigh; strong limbs with short cannons, flat, hard bone and well-shaped, hard, dark hooves; silky feather, not over-heavy and ending in a prominent tuft at the fetlock; long, silky, flowing mane and tail.

upwards of 16 stone (224lb/101kg) – back
down. It is much used for pony trekking
and makes a fine general-purpose riding
pony, well able to carry an adult. Pure-
breds can be seen taking part successfully
in a number of competitive sports,
including driving and dressage. Crossed
with the Thoroughbred the Highland
makes an excellent hunter and more than
one successful three-day event horse has
had Highland blood in its veins.

INTERESTING FACTS

One of the most striking features of the
Highland is its colouring, particularly the
various shades of dun: yellow, golden, mouse,
cream and fox (yellow dun is believed to have
been the breed's original colour). Most ponies
show at least one of the characteristics of the
primitive horse, i.e. a dorsal eel-stripe and
zebra markings on the legs. These markings
testify to the antiquity of the breed.

▌ ABOVE
Highland Ponies are noted for the beauty of their
coat colouring – including the whole range of duns
– and for the silky texture of their abundant manes
and tails.

▌ BELOW
Versatility is one of the most valuable
characteristics of the breed, which will haul
timber as easily as it will carry a rider to hounds
or go in harness.

▌ OPPOSITE TOP
The Highland Pony's
head is broad between
the eyes, short from
eyes to muzzle and
well-carried on a
strong, arched neck.
The eyes have a kind
expression.

▌ OPPOSITE
Moulded by its harsh
natural environment,
the breed is strong,
hardy, long lived and
economical to feed. It
is eminently sure-
footed over the most
treacherous terrain.

Shetland

Named after the remote group of islands situated to the far north-east of mainland Scotland and in the same northern latitude as south Greenland, the Shetland Pony is the smallest of the British native breeds. Its origins are uncertain but there have certainly been ponies in the Shetlands for many centuries and it may

▮ LEFT
The Shetland's profuse growth of mane and tail afford valuable protection from the severe weather of its northern homeland.

BREED DESCRIPTION

Height Not exceeding 40 inches (102cm) at three years or under. Not exceeding 42 inches (107cm) at four years or over.

Colour Any colour except spotted.

Conformation Small, well-carried head with broad forehead, bold, dark, intelligent eyes, small, erect ears and broad muzzle with wide open nostrils; strong, deep body with short back and muscular loins; broad, strong hindquarters; strong limbs, with good, flat bone and short cannons; tough, round, well-shaped feet.

---

well trace back to far more distant times.

Small of stature, it is nevertheless immensely strong – one of the strongest equine animals, in relation to size, in the world. Wonderfully well adapted to the vagaries of the islands' northern climate and the poor quality grazing, the Shetland is inherently hardy. Its action is free and straight, with a characteristic lift to its joints – the result of centuries of traversing rough, rocky or heather-covered terrain. An integral part of the lives of the

islanders, the ponies have traditionally been used both under saddle and as pack animals, carrying everything from grain to peat for fuel. They were formerly much in demand for coal mining, their small size and great strength making them perfect for work underground. Breeding flourished, though there was little attempt at selective breeding before the middle of the nineteenth century.

The Shetland has also found favour far from its native islands as a children's riding pony. It can be strong-willed but it is intelligent and responds to correct handling. With its active paces and manoeuvrability, it makes a particularly good driving pony and can be seen competing right up to international level.

▮ LEFT
Short-legged and stocky, the breed is noted for its great strength in relation to its diminutive size.

▌ LEFT
Shetlands are very active little ponies and take part with great enthusiasm in Shetland "Grand Nationals", which raise money for charity.

▌ BELOW
In spring the Shetland begins to shed its thick winter coat designed to keep out extremes of wet and cold.

Stop this is dangerous

▌ ABOVE
Shetland Ponies can be wilful, but in the hands of a competent child they make good riding ponies.

▌ RIGHT
Centuries of living on rough, rock-strewn terrain have made the ponies both active and sure-footed. Their feet are well-shaped and extremely hard.

INTERESTING FACTS

In winter the Shetland Pony grows a double coat as protection against the inclement climate of its native home. The coat has "guard hairs", which shed rain and keep the pony's skin completely dry, however severe the weather. The mane and tail are profuse.

143

Welsh Cob

The Welsh Cob (designated Section D in the Welsh Pony and Cob Society Stud Book) is derived from the Welsh Mountain Pony, of which it is, in essence, a larger version. It traces back at least to the twelfth century when eastern-type horses were brought back by the Crusaders and crossed with the local ponies. Subsequently infusions of Yorkshire Coach Horse, Norfolk Roadster and Arab blood were made.

Tough, sound, spirited and courageous, yet with an amenable temperament, the

BREED DESCRIPTION

Height Above 13.2hh – usually 14.2 – 15.2hh.

Colour Any, except piebald and skewbald.

Conformation Quality, pony head with bold, widely set eyes and neat, well-set ears; long, well-carried neck; strong, well laid-back shoulders; strong, deep, muscular body; muscular hindquarters; short, powerful limbs with long, strong forearms, strong, muscular second thighs, large, flat joints and well-shaped feet.

INTERESTING FACTS

By crossing Welsh Mountain Pony mares with small Welsh Cobs breeders produced the Welsh Pony of Cob Type (Section C in the Stud Book), a smaller version of the Cob and a marvellous all-round riding and driving pony. It shares all the characteristics of its larger cousin, but does not stand over 13.2hh. Like the Cob, it was formerly much used by hill farmers and also to transport slate from the mines of North Wales. After World War II it was in danger of becoming extinct, but its numbers have since recovered and nowadays it enjoys popularity as a trekking pony, a small hunter and as a driving pony.

Welsh Cob was traditionally used for all manner of heavy work on the hill farms, being equally at home in harness and under saddle, and it formed an integral part of life in Wales. It was also formerly much in demand by the army, particularly for pulling guns and other heavy military equipment. The Welsh Cob was also used for the mounted infantry. Possessed of active paces and great stamina, the Welsh Cob is renowned above all for its spectacular trotting action, inherited no doubt from the Norfolk Roadster. Indeed, up until 1918, when stallion licensing was introduced, breeding stock was selected by means of trotting matches. Nowadays, not surprisingly, the breed enjoys notable success in the sport of carriage driving.

▌ OPPOSITE ABOVE
The Welsh Cob is described by the breed society as the embodiment of strength and hardiness. The action is straight, free and forceful. The whole foreleg is extended from the shoulders and as far forward as possible in all paces, with the hocks well flexed, producing powerful leverage. A quality head, depth through the girth and strong limbs, with an abundance of flat bone, are prerequisites of this sturdy breed.

Unique among the British Mountain and Moorland breeds, the Cob has no upper height limit, but whatever its size it should retain true pony characteristics – its quality head testifying to its Welsh Mountain Pony ancestry.

When crossed with the Thoroughbred (particularly the second cross) the Welsh Cob produces excellent competition horses and is in great demand today.

▌ LEFT
The Welsh Cob is a popular attraction in the show ring, as well as being a marvellous all-round performer in competitive sports.

Caspian

In 1965 an exciting discovery was made in northern Iran, in a remote, mountainous region not far from the Caspian Sea. Some three dozen miniature horses, no taller than a small pony but with the outward characteristics of a diminutive horse, were found. Detailed scientific examination revealed that these little horses had certain physical characteristics that did not match those of other horses: an extra full-sized molar on each side of the upper jaw; a scapula that was a different shape from that usually found in equine animals, and a slightly different formation of the three parietal bones in the head.

The Caspian Pony, as it has become known, is believed to be the direct descendant of the earliest equine animals that roamed the region around 3,000 BC. Bones have been excavated in Iran that point to the existence in the area of a very similar small horse at that period, a seal in the British Museum shows King Darius riding in a chariot drawn by horses of

Caspian type, and other artefacts of the period exist depicting similar small horses. It is thought possible that the Caspian is a far-off ancestor of the Arabian.

For many centuries the Caspian was mysteriously "lost". After its re-discovery a careful breeding programme was set up at studs in order to safeguard its future. Caspian Ponies can now be found in a number of European countries as well as Australia, New Zealand and the United States.

The Caspian is extremely hardy, and possesses great speed and endurance as well as a kind temperament. It has dense bone and exceptionally hard, tough feet, which do not require shoeing. It makes a good riding pony and despite its small size has remarkable jumping ability.

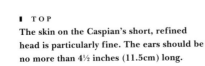

■ TOP
The skin on the Caspian's short, refined head is particularly fine. The ears should be no more than 4½ inches (11.5cm) long.

■ ABOVE
On account of its small size the breed is described as a pony, although it has all the attributes of a miniature horse.

Despite its lack of height, the Caspian has wonderful natural action; it can keep up with a horse at walk, trot and canter. Even at this early age the foal shows tremendous length of stride.

Connemara

LEFT
The Connemara's beautiful head possesses
great refinement. Grey is the breed's
predominant colour.

Elegant, hardy, intelligent, possessed of
tremendous agility and jumping prowess,
the Connemara is arguably the best
performance pony in the world. It is
Ireland's only indigenous breed; it takes
its name from the wild, rocky region on
the western seaboard of Ireland where
ponies have existed, in one form or
another, since ancient times.

How this paragon among ponies
developed is unclear. One theory is that it
is descended from Barb and Spanish
horses introduced into the west of Ireland
as early as the sixth century BC, when the
Celts overran the whole of Europe. These
horses would then have been crossed with
the indigenous stock. Also, during
subsequent centuries of trade between the
west coast of Ireland and the Iberian
peninsula it is highly likely that quantities
of horses would have been imported. The
breed undoubtedly does show signs of
Spanish and eastern blood to this day. The
suggestion that the Connemara is
descended from horses of the Spanish
Armada that swam ashore after being
shipwrecked in 1588 is nowadays dismissed
by most experts as mere fancy!

Arab stallions are known to have been
imported by landowners during the
middle of the nineteenth century, but it is
impossible to say what influence, if any,
they had on the Connemara. During the
latter part of the century, however, Welsh

BREED DESCRIPTION

Height Not exceeding 14.2hh.

Colour Predominantly grey but also brown,
dun, black and occasionally chestnut and
roan.

Conformation Short head, often with
slightly dished profile, with broad forehead,
dark, full eyes, small ears; long, arched neck
giving good length of rein; well-sloped
shoulders; deep, compact body; strong
hindquarters with high-set tail; good strong
limbs with short cannons and plenty of bone
below the knee; strong, sound feet.

RIGHT
Excellent conformation - notably the well-
sloped shoulders - make the Connemara a
superb riding pony, possessed of strength,
free-going movement and superb balance.

Little Model was one of many part-bred Connemaras who have achieved great success in the competitive disciplines. By a Thoroughbred stallion out of a Connemara mare, Little Model, a grey, was originally trained for circus work. The British dressage rider Mrs V.D.S. Williams spent a good deal of time persuading him to "unlearn" various tricks before he could concentrate on Grand Prix work. Together they competed in the 1960 Olympics, finishing in a very creditable eleventh place. The following year they were third in the European Championships – Britain's first placing in a dressage championship. Sadly, because he was such a bad traveller, Little Model never competed abroad again although he enjoyed many successes at home.

I ABOVE
Connemaras in their natural habitat of western Ireland.

blood was certainly introduced and did play a part: one of the Welsh stallions, Prince Llewellyn, sired Dynamite out of a native mare. Dynamite in turn sired Cannon Ball (foaled in 1904), who is the first stallion listed in the Connemara Stud Book. Other attempts to "improve" the breed included the use of Thoroughbred, Hackney and Clydesdale blood.

Finally, in 1923, the Connemara Pony Breeders' Society was founded in Galway. It had the backing of the Department of Agriculture and the intention was to improve the breed from within, by seeking out the best type of mare and an appropriate number of similar quality

stallions to use as foundation stock. The result of these efforts is an outstanding, quality pony of fixed type, courageous but sensible, able to excel in virtually all sports, from show jumping and three-day eventing to dressage and driving. When crossed with the Thoroughbred it produces a top-class performance horse.

I BELOW
Traditional pony power: carting seaweed in Galway.

I ABOVE
As a ridden pony the Connemara cannot be bettered. Spirited but sensible, courageous but kind, it is an ideal mount for children and adults alike.

Fjord

Norway's unusual looking Fjord Pony is believed to have inhabited Norway and probably other parts of Scandinavia since prehistoric times. At a quick glance it is not unlike the Przewalski's Horse (the Asiatic Wild Horse) in appearance, though the head is much less heavy and "primitive", being more pony-like in size and shape. Ponies resembling the Fjord are depicted in Viking art. They can be seen fighting, a pastime which was also popular in Iceland and which may have been engaged in for sport, as a form of performance testing or, probably, a combination of both.

Hundreds if not thousands of years spent in a mountainous habitat have

produced a pony that is perfectly adapted to its environment. Sturdy and muscular, the Fjord has short, strong legs with good joints and hard, sound feet. Down the centuries its inherent sure-footedness, strength, soundness and tremendous stamina have made it an invaluable

BREED DESCRIPTION

Height 13 – 14hh.

Colour Most shades of dun with a black dorsal eel-stripe and, often, zebra markings on the legs.

Conformation Pony-type head with broad forehead and small ears; muscular neck; strong, deep body; fairly low-set tail; short, strong limbs with good joints, short cannons and plenty of bone; hard, sound feet.

helpmate to farmers. Used to coping with severe weather conditions and undaunted by the most rugged terrain, it also proved the perfect pack-pony for use on mountain trails.

Nowadays the Fjord Pony can be found in a number of countries outside Scandinavia, including Germany, Denmark and England. It makes a good general-purpose riding pony and also goes well in harness.

▌ LEFT
Although its natural environment is the mountains, the adaptable Fjord can be found in many other types of country, where it is valued both for its attractive appearance and its performance ability.

▌ OPPOSITE TOP
The Fjord has a true pony head, with small ears, large, wide-set eyes and a small muzzle which is lighter in colour than the rest of the coat.

▌ OPPOSITE
The pony's stocky build testifies to its great strength. Deep through the girth and with a particularly muscular neck and strong legs, it is a great little worker in areas not accessible to machines.

▌ LEFT
The striking colouring of the mane and tail, with their black and silver hair, is unique to the Fjord Pony.

▌ RIGHT
Fjords make excellent driving ponies. They have a kind, willing temperament but are active movers and, like all mountain breeds, exceptionally sure-footed.

INTERESTING FACTS

One of the most distinctive features of the Fjord Pony is its unusual mane and tail colouring. Both mane and tail have black hairs in the centre, with silver on the outside. The stiff mane is traditionally cut in a curve with the dark inner hair standing higher than the outer silver hair.

Types

Horses and ponies with unusual or exotic coat colours and patterns have occurred throughout history and have usually been highly prized by man, regardless of their breeding. In recent times registers or stud books have been opened in some countries for the most popular of these colour types – in fact some now qualify for the title "breeds". The term "breed" is used to describe horses who have been bred selectively over a period of time and who have, as a result, developed fixed characteristics. Horses belonging to a particular breed have their pedigrees recorded in a stud book. The term "type" describes a horse bred for a particular purpose, such as hunting. Any number of permutations can be (and are) used to produce a horse suitable for riding to hounds and hunters cannot therefore be described as a breed. Horse and pony types, although few in number compared with the established breeds, nevertheless have an important role to play in the world of leisure riding.

Palomino

Throughout history man has prized horses with golden-coloured coats. Horses with this striking colouring are depicted in works of art, often dating back many centuries, from Asia, Japan and a number of European countries. Golden horses are referred to in Homer's *The Iliad* and in Norse legend. In Spain Queen Isabella,

BREED DESCRIPTION

Height The registry of the Palomino Horse Breeders of America (PHBA) admits horses standing between 14 and 17hh.

Colour Body colour of a newly minted gold coin, with variations from light to dark. The skin is usually grey, black, brown or motley, without underlying pink skin or spots except on the face or legs. Black, hazel or brown eyes. White mane and tail with not more than 15 per cent dark, sorrel or chestnut hairs. Dorsal stripe and zebra stripes not permitted.

Conformation To be eligible for registration with the PHBA a Palomino must show refinement of head, bone, and general structure appropriate to the breeds recognized by the PHBA and be suitable for carrying Western or English equipment. It must show no pony or draught horse characteristics.

sponsor of Columbus, encouraged their breeding, as a result of which they are often referred to in that country as "Isabellas".

There are various suggestions as to the derivation of the word Palomino, now used to describe golden horses. The most likely is that it comes from Juan de Palomino, who received a horse of this colouring from Cortès. Other theories are that it comes from the name of a Spanish grape or from the word *paloma*, meaning dove. Palomino colouring features in a number of breeds, therefore the term Palomino refers to a colour type, not a specific breed.

▌ PREVIOUS PAGE OPPOSITE
A Paint horse with totiano markings.

▌ PREVIOUS PAGE
Typical Palomino colouring.

▌ ABOVE
Palominos always have a white mane and tail. For registration purposes the head must be of true riding horse proportions, with no pony or draught characteristics.

▌ LEFT
This Quarter Horse is an admirable example of the requirements of the PHBA, which call for a body colour "of a newly minted gold coin".

■ RIGHT
Palominos, like this
English pony, are
found all over the
world and do not have
to be of any particular
breed to qualify for
registration as such.

■ BELOW RIGHT
Golden-coloured
horses have been
prized throughout
history and in all parts
of the world. These
two were
photographed in
France.

INTERESTING FACTS

Palomino colouring occurs in a number of
breeds. In the United States they include the
Morgan Horse, the Quarter Horse, the
Saddlebred and the Tennessee Walking Horse,
while in Britain there are some striking looking
Palominos among the Welsh Ponies and Cobs.

cremello. Cross a Palomino with a sorrel
and the chances are still only 50 per cent –
and any Palomino colouring that is
achieved may be too poor to be eligible for
most Palomino societies. Cross a Palomino
with any other colour and the chances of
producing a Palomino foal diminish.

Despite the uncertainties involved in
breeding for colour, Palomino horses
retain their age-old appeal. Being good all-
round riding horses – conformation
should never be sacrificed for the sake of
colour – they can be seen taking part in all
kinds of activities, from cutting horse
events to trail riding.

They may occur in many parts of the
world, but Palomino horses are particularly
associated with North America, where they
were introduced by the Spanish
Conquistadores. The origin of this type of
colouring is uncertain but it is thought to
have come from the Arab – though it is not
found nowadays in the pure-bred Arabian
horse. One of the intriguing, if frustrating,
aspects of Palomino horses is that they do
not "breed true", in other words there is no
sure-fire way of ensuring Palomino
colouring in a foal. It is all a question of
genetics and the genetics of equine coat
colouring is a complicated subject,
involving dominant and recessive genes.
Put simply, mate a Palomino to a Palomino
and there is only a 50 per cent chance of a
Palomino foal. There is a 25 per cent
chance that the foal will be sorrel (a bright
chestnut) and the same chance of the
result being a pseudo-albino, known as a

Appaloosa

The spotted coat colouring of the
American Appaloosa traces back to stock
imported by the Spanish Conquistadores.
Spotted horses became particularly prized
by the Nez Percé Indian tribe who lived in
the region that is now northern Idaho,
north-east Oregon and south-east
Washington. The word Appaloosa is
derived from Palouse country, an area
named after the Palouse river.

The Nez Percé are said to be the first
Indian tribe to have practised systematic
breeding of horses. Following the defeat
of the Indians by the US army during the
latter half of the nineteenth century, the
horses which escaped slaughter became
scattered. It was not until the 1920s that
efforts were made to re-establish the
Appaloosa horse, using the descendants of
those which survived as a basis. In 1938
the Appaloosa Horse Club was founded in
Oregon. Its objectives were to collect
records and historical data relating to the
origin of the Appaloosa, to preserve,
improve and standardize the breed and to
set up a register for approved animals.

The re-establishment of the Appaloosa
has been a great success and today the
breed is widely used in all types of Western
riding, for endurance riding and in the
show ring in both hunter and jumper
classes. Appaloosas are mainly associated

BREED DESCRIPTION

Height Around 14.2 – 15.2hh.

Colour Spotted. The skin is mottled (especially noticeable around the nostrils and genitalia).

Conformation The Appaloosa is a compact stamp of horse with a well-shaped neck, short, strong back, powerful hindquarters and strong limbs with extremely good, hard feet.

INTERESTING FACTS

In America gaited spotted horses, that is those who show the ability to perform an intermediate gait other than the trot (such as the rack, foxtrot, running walk or pace) are termed Walkaloosas. To qualify for registration with the Walkaloosa Horse Association, which was founded in 1983, a horse must meet one of three criteria: either be the progeny of a registered Walkaloosa stallion and mare, or show Appaloosa colouring and demonstrate an intermediate gait other than trot, or be the product of verifiable Appaloosa (colour) and Paso, Foxtrotter or Tennessee Walker blood. The Walkaloosa's colouring is typical of that found in the Appaloosa, including white sclera round the eyes. Coat patterns include, but are not limited to, leopard, blanket and snowflake. The Walkaloosa, like the Appaloosa, is noted for its kind, sensible nature and makes an outstanding pleasure and trail horse.

▌ LEFT
This horse and rider, decked out in traditional style, recall the time when spotted horses were the preferred mounts of the Nez Percé Indians.

▌ FAR LEFT
Spotted horses are popular in many countries outside the United States. There is a thriving Appaloosa society in Britain – this horse was photographed at the Royal Windsor Horse Show.

with the United States but they are also found in many other countries.

There are five main Appaloosa coat patterns: leopard – white colouring over the loins and hips with dark, round or egg-shaped spots; snowflake – dark spots all over a white body but usually dominant over the hips; blanket – white area over the hips without dark spots in the white; marble – mottled all over the body; frost – white specks with a dark background. Other distinguishing features include white sclera round the eyes and, often, vertical black and white stripes on the hooves. The mane and tail tend to be quite sparse.

▌ LEFT
Noted for its strong limbs and the excellence of its feet, the Appaloosa makes a good endurance riding horse.

Paint Horse

Horses with broken coloured coats (also known as piebalds and skewbalds) are found all over the world, though they are particularly associated with the North American Indian.

In America a horse with this type of colouring may be registered either as a Paint Horse or as a Pinto, depending on the horse meeting certain criteria. The American Paint Horse Association was founded in 1962 to provide a register for horses with individual, colourful patterns of contrasting light and dark hair and skin, and distinctive stock-type conformation. To qualify for registration with the APHA

horses must be bred from registered American Paint Horses, registered American Quarter Horses or registered Thoroughbreds and must meet a minimum colour requirement. A horse with a predominantly solid-coloured coat must have a definite "natural" Paint marking, which is defined as an area of solid white hair with some underlying,

unpigmented skin. A horse with a mainly white hair coat must have a contrasting area of colour with some underlying, pigmented skin. The contrasting areas should be visible at the time the foal is born and at the time of registration.

The APHA maintains two registries, the Regular and the Breeding Stock. To be eligible for inclusion in the Regular

▌ TOP LEFT
This Paint horse has tobiano markings: dark colouring on the flanks, a "shield" down the neck and chest and white legs.

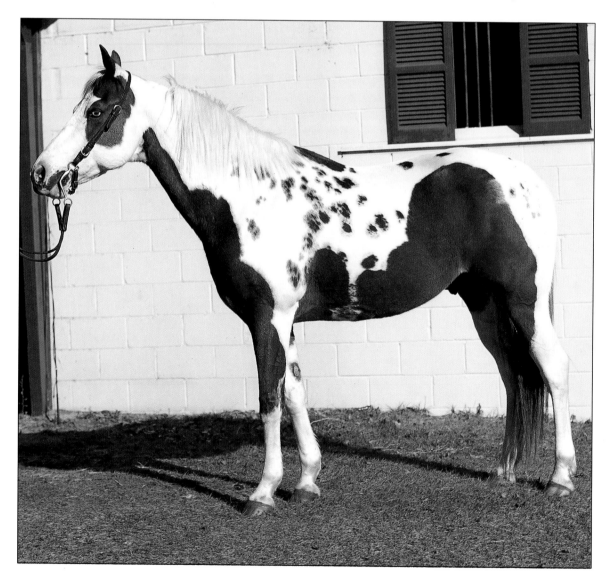

▌ OPPOSITE
Paint horses have always been associated with the American West. The horse on the left is an overo with a bald face.

▌ LEFT
The characteristic shape and build of the Paint horse is that of the stock horse: good overall riding horse conformation and a sturdy, compact appearance.

Like the Paint horse, the Pinto has overo or tobiano colouring (this horse is a tobiano). For registration purposes, Pintos are divided by conformation type.

Registry the foal must have at least one "natural" Paint marking which is a minimum of 2 inches (5cm) in diameter. If a horse does not meet the required colour requirement but meets the other registration requirements (for example a solid-coloured foal resulting from a mating between two registered American Paint Horses), it may be entered in the Breeding Stock Registry.

The spectrum of coat colours in the Paint Horse encompasses all of the tones known in the horse world. The patterns range from almost total colour with a minimal amount of white to almost total white with minimal colour. The patterns are distinguished by the location of colour on the horse, the two major ones being overo and tobiano.

Overo horses have the following characteristics: the white usually will not cross the back of the horse between the withers and the tail; generally at least one and often all four legs will be dark; generally the white is irregular, rather scattered or splashy, and is often referred to as calico; head markings are often bald-faced, apron-faced or bonnet-faced; the tail is usually one colour.

Tobiano horses have the following characteristics: the dark colour will usually cover one or both flanks; generally all four legs will be white, at least below the hocks and knees; generally the spots are regular and distinct as ovals or round patterns which extend down over the neck and chest, giving the appearance of a shield; head markings are like those of a solid-coloured horse – solid colour or with a blaze, stripe, star or snip; the tail usually displays two colours.

Horses with overo and tobiano characteristics are called toveros.

Knabstrupter

Spotted horses have been known – and have often been highly prized – since ancient times. They can be seen in early Chinese art and there were spotted strains of the Noriker (Austria's old-established light draught breed) and the Spanish horses which were so influential in the development of many of the world's modern breeds. Denmark's once-famous Knabstrup is of Spanish ancestry and dates back to the time of the Napoleonic Wars. At that time a spotted mare named Flaebehoppen was acquired by a butcher called Flaebe (hence her name). Flaebehoppen, an exceptionally fast mare possessed of great endurance, was bred by her next owner, Judge Lunn, to Frederiksborg horses and founded a line of spotted horses. Named the Knabstrup, after Lunn's estate, this strain was rather less substantial than the Frederiksborg but

BREED DESCRIPTION

Height Around 15.2 – 16hh.

Colour Mainly white, with brown or black spots of varying size over the body, head and legs.

Conformation Variable, but the best examples have reasonably good overall conformation, with a kind, intelligent head. The mane and tail are usually sparse, as in the majority of spotted horses.

INTERESTING FACTS

The breed's remarkable talents as a circus horse were demonstrated in America not so long ago when a centre-ring attraction consisted of a large Bengal tiger riding a Knabstrup horse. The horse wore protective harness – in case the big cat slipped and decided to hang on with his claws!

was tough and sound and, because of its attractive markings, became popular as a circus horse. Subsequent crossings back to the Frederiksborg reduced the number of pure-bred Knabstrup horses but examples of the breed are still to be found, though not in anywhere near the numbers of the American Appaloosa.

TOP LEFT
The mottled skin colouring of the lips and muzzle, so typical of all spotted horses, can be clearly seen on this Knabstrup.

LEFT
The characteristic white body hair with all-over dark spots, together with its intelligent, kind nature, made the Knabstrup a popular circus horse.

Index

Acknowledgements

The author would like to thank the many individuals and breed societies who kindly provided information for use in this book, particularly: The American Morgan Horse Association, Inc; The American Paint Horse Association; The American Saddlebred Horse Association, Inc; The British Spotted Pony Society; Vivienne Burdon; The Cleveland Bay Horse Society; The Clydesdale Horse Society of Great Britain and Ireland; The Exmoor Pony Society; The Hackney Horse Society; The Haflinger Society of Great Britain; The Highland Pony Society; The Irish Draught Horse Society (GB); Sylvia Loch (author of *The Royal Horse of Europe*, J. A. Allen, 1986); The Lusitano Breed Society of Great Britain; The Palomino Horse Association of America, Inc; The Pinto Horse Association of America, Inc; Valerie Russell; The Suffolk Horse Society; The Walkaloosa Horse Association; The Walking Horse Owners' Association of America, Inc; The Welsh Pony and Cob Society.

We are also grateful to the following for allowing their horses, ponies and stables to be photographed:

Arab – Sariah Arabians, Dorking, Surrey
Barb – Haras Regional de Marrakech, Morocco
Thoroughbred – Mrs M Blackburn, c/o Catherston Stud, Whitchurch, Hampshire
Anglo-Arab – Woodlander Stud, Raglan, Gwent
Danish Warmblood – Catherston Stud, Whitchurch, Hampshire
Ariègeois – Bob Langrish, photographer
Camargue – Laurent Serre, Camargue, France
Norman Cob – Haras National Le Lion d'Angers, Loire, France
Selle Français – Haras National Le Lion d'Angers, Loire, France
French Trotter – Haras National Le Lion d'Angers, Loire, France
Breton – Haras National Le Lion d'Angers, Loire, France
Percheron – Haras National Le Lion d'Angers, Loire, France
Hanoverian – Mrs S Bray, Nuneaton, Warwickshire
Oldenburg – I Brendel, Trenthide, Dorset
Westphalian – Marlow Building Co Ltd, Marlow, Buckinghamshire
Hackney – Georgina Turner, Ipswich, Essex
Shire – Lingwood Shire, Brentwood, Essex
Suffolk – Randy Hiscock, Shaftsbury, Dorset
Icelandic – Edda Hestar, Salisbury, Wiltshire
Friesian – Harrods, London

Gelderland – Mr Luetzow, Wokingham, Berkshire
Holstein – Mr Luetzow, Wokingham, Berkshire
Dutch Warmblood – Mrs C Hughes, Doncaster
Shagya Arab – Sonia Lindsay, Okehampton, Devon
Akhal-Teke – Viscountess Bury, Plumpton, Sussex
Budenny – Mrs Marcus, Beoley, Redditch, Hereford & Worcester (action)
Don – Russian Horse Society, Epsom, Surrey (standing) & Mrs June Connolly, Droitwich, West Midlands (action)
Kabardin – Mrs June Connolly, Droitwich, West Midlands
Orlov – George Bowman Jnr, Penrith, Lancashire
Vladmir – Russian Horse Society,

Epsom, Surrey
North Swedish – Jan Gyllensten, photographer, Sweden

USA
Morgan – Betty Gray, Orange Lake, Florida
Quarter Horse – Quiet Oaks Farm, Ocala, Florida & Derby Daze Farm, Ocala, Florida
Saddlebred – Boca Raton Equestrian Centre, Del Ray Beach
Standardbred – David McDuffee & Tom Walsh Jnr, South Florida Trotting Center
Missouri Foxtrotter – Sandy Hart, Winter Haven, Florida
Tennessee Walker – Mrs Carol Worsham, Dunnellon, Florida
Palomino – Holmes Quarter Horses, Brandon, Florida
Appaloosa – Classic Acres Farm, Ocala, Florida
Paint – Brooke Hamlin, Ocala, Florida
Mustang – Cindy Bowman, Dunnellon, Florida
Peruvian Paso – Annette Ward, Alachua, Florida

PONIES
Haflinger – Millslade Farm Stud, Bridgwater, Somerset
Exmoor – Mrs J Freeman, Wareside, Hertfordshire
Shetland – Mr & Mrs E House, Bincombe Shetlands, Bridgwater, Somerset
DalesWareside, Hertfordshire
Shetland – Mr & Mrs E House, Bincombe Shetlands, Bridgwater, Somerset
Dales – Mrs B Powell, Farnham, Surrey
New Forest – Shirley Young, Salisbury, Wiltshire
Connemara & Welsh Sec B – Miss S Clark, Dorking, Surrey
Fjord – Mrs Murray, Ottery St Mary, Devon
Caspian – Henden Caspian Stud, Chippenham, Wiltshire
Knabstrub – Mrs Ann Peruzzi-Smith, Diss, Norfolk